**THE
WALL
STREET
JOURNAL
BOOK
OF WIT**

THE WALL STREET JOURNAL BOOK OF WIT

A 10 Year Treasury of
Thousands of Highly
Quotable Rhymes,
Daffynitions and Quips

Edited By
CHARLES PRESTON

DOW JONES-IRWIN
Homewood, Illinois 60430

© DOW JONES-IRWIN, 1980

ISBN 0-87094-227-1

Library of Congress Catalog Card No.

Printed in the United States of America

1 2 3 4 5 6 7 8 9 0 8 7 6 5 4 3 2 1

Introduction

Moments of Truth

The humorist's role is to observe and comment on our follies. There are two postures available to the comic commentator:

1. Chastise the erring by focusing on and often exaggerating their behavior. The comic appears to say: "Hah! Look what a fool you are."

2. Recognize—and empathize with—human fallibility. Here, the comic observation is: "Oh, dear. How he carries on, but this helps me to see some of myself. Hmmm . . ."

Pepper and Salt is guided by the latter empathy. As a daily newspaper column, Pepper and Salt is in a position to comment while the irony is hot. (When the energy crisis first loomed, we warned about acting fuelish; when clones made the headlines, Pepper and Salt contributors cautioned us about cloning around.)

Though we respond to news events and affairs of the world, it is the ordinary day-to-day life that accounts for the corn in our pepper mill. PTA meetings, supermarket checkout lines, computers and all sorts of ordinary things furnish most of the inspiration for our anecdotes, epigrams and verse.

We have long agreed with poet Phyllis McGinley's observation that the purpose of light verse is to shed light. It is "the thrust of thought" that is primary—and we sometimes let the meter slide in order to secure the meaning.

This anthology, spanning almost two decades of poetic and epigrammatic commentary, seeks to cool contemporary fervor and should lead to a sympathetic evaluation of our risible behavior. Translation: Distance makes the difference. Though he may not have thought it was funny back then, the fortyish balding executive should be able to appreciate the comic comments on his long-haired communal living in the 60s.

Grouped in categories and described by subject headings, the verse, anecdotes, epigrams and daffynitions are easily accessible for the speechwriter, storyteller and the general reader.

Public speakers for many years have looked to the Pepper and Salt column for condiments to enliven their speeches. Here, for the first time, is a major collection of that humor.

Acknowledgement

Every week over 1,000 contributions pour into our Pepper & Salt shaker from every state and overseas. In the present collection are the works of more than 100 writers. My thanks to these faithful contributors.

And a special thanks to the editorial page staff of The Wall Street Journal, with a particular nod toward Eric Lloyd and Pat Dolce.

For editorial assistance, layout and research, I'm grateful to Charles Preston, Paul Jerr, Anne S. Ryan, and Daisy Brown.

"Go ask your mother."

Marital Manners

"The head of the household? Oh boy, are you gonna get me in trouble!"

Believer
"Boy!" the husband sighed as he settled down with a cocktail on his return from work. "You'll never believe what a dopey thing I did today!" "Honestly, Herb," his wife said reproachfully, "I wish you'd have a little more confidence in me!"
—Edward Stevenson.

Facts of Life
Marriage is a great teacher. And much of what it teaches you don't need to know unless you get married.
—Robert Fuoss.

Posting Their Banes
Lines of disagreement
Today have grown quite thin.
Some marriages that break up
Were barely broken in.
—Gail Cooke.

Write on:
The permanence of the
   marriage pact
Depends on how couples
   plan it;
With some the vows are
   written on sand,
While others take them for
   granite.
—George O. Ludcke.

Marital Manners

Nagging Truth
One couple I know
Are birds of a feather,
Jolly and gracious—
Except when together.
      —A. S. Flaumenhaft.

Marital Manners
[*"News Note: Study shows
that marriage instruction
course reduces likelihood of
divorce."*]
Premarital indoctrination
For prospective groom and
    bride
Alters their egos in such a
    way
That they are fit to be tied.
      —George O. Ludcke.

Marital Problem
"I don't understand," said
the marriage counselor to his
client. "You say you don't
trust your husband because
he's a jogger?"
"Anyone," said the
woman, "who would say he
runs 10 miles a day, with his
muscles aching, his heart
pounding and his lungs on
fire—because it makes him
feel good—he'd lie about
other things as well!"
      —Robert Orben.

Wedlock vs. Deadlock
Some solutions, I've
concluded,

Put the horse behind the
    carriage;
Couples open with each other
Don't need an "open
    marriage".
      —Rosemarie Williamson.

Wifely Logic
The toothpaste he forgets to
    cap;
For neatness he cares not a
    rap.
At night I listen to him snore;
At parties often he's a bore.
But what care I what faults
    has he
As long as he puts up with
    me.
      —Lea Zwettler.

No Embellishment?
You used to compliment me
    often—
I never had to guess;
But now I ask, "Am I
    attractive?"
And you simply answer,
    "Yes."
      —Rosemarie Williamson.

Romeo Revisited
It is darn aggravating to
    admit that
When her sole source of
    tender, loving care
Gets that gleam in his eye
    right after dinner,
His object is a soft, reclining
    chair.
      —Fred W. Norman.

Wistful Shrinking
Darling, you are always right!
I'm the one who isn't bright.
Wall Street expert, you can
    tell
When to buy and when to
    sell,
You beat colds and double
    chins
Eating proteins, vitamins.
Luggage, toasters, wristwatch,
    car—
You know where the bargains
    are.
When I spurn your good
    advice
Later I must pay the price.
Though my love for you is
    strong,
Sweetheart, can't you once be
    wrong?
      —Edith Ogutsch.

Ritual
"What makes you think
your wife worships you?"
"Every morning she serves
me burnt offerings."
      —Shelby Friedman.

Ballot Boxed
My wife and I, on equal
    terms,
Live happily together.
It's my decision what to do;
She just determines whether.
      —Robert W. Campbell.

Marital Manners

Daffynitions

German bigamist: frau loader.
—Raymond J. Cvikota.

Matrimony: the first union to defy management.
—Paul Harwitz.

Payoff

About those bonds of
   matrimony
There's something that's for
   sure:
To add up to something
   special
You must wait for them to
   mature.
—Dorothy B. Bennett.

Standoff

The secret of happy marriage,
Long years without a hitch,
Is known by those partners
Who'd rather fight than
   switch!
—Ruth M. Walsh.

Candid Comment

A wife who has ambitions for her husband is often the kind of woman who will drive a man to distinction.
—Daisy Brown.

Kids

"Mom . . . you suppose we might put a phone in this corner?"

Kids

Putdown

Little Eddie knelt by the side of his bed and began, "Our Father, who art in heaven—"

"Speak up, dear," interrupted his mother. "I can't hear you."

"I wasn't talking to you," replied Eddie.

Name Dropper

A lively little boy was creating much commotion in the waiting room of a busy bus terminal. Attempting to divert him, a kindly matron asked, "What's your name, dear?"

"Johnny."

"And your full name?" the lady persisted.

"I'm not sure," replied the lad, looking puzzled, "but I think it's Johnny Be-Quiet."

Goal Line

Two small boys were comparing notes on their families. When the subject of grandparents was brought up, one little fellow said, "I think your grandmother's very nice —but why is she always reading the Bible?"

"I've wondered the same thing," the other boy replied. "So I asked my big brother. And he said granny is cramming for her finals!"

Big Deal!

The FBI recently announced that it has over seventy million fingerprints. So has every home containing small children.

—Honey Greer.

Uncounted Blessing

The mother was tucking her little daughter into bed. "Goodnight, dear," she whispered, "and God bless you."

"Mommy," said the tot soberly, "did I sneeze?"

—Jennifer Lonoff.

Go Between

What's the best age for
    children?
Here's my favorite by far:
Too old to cry at night,
Too young to borrow the car!
        —Dorothy B. Bennett.

Get the Picture?

To the many virtues of
    children,
There is another trait I must
    add;
They never try to entertain
    you
With movies of their mother
    and dad!
        —R. Kuchenbecker.

Proving Their Metal

All kids in braces
Feel quite certain
They're raised behind
An iron curtain.
        —Jean B. Chisholm.

Enlightened Parent

It's time, I thought uneasily,
To summon the kiddies to
    my knee
For a private talk about bird
    and bee,
And oooooooh!
What they told me!
        —Ethel Jacobson.

Astronomical Note

Having a famous father very often leads to a total eclipse of the son.

—Robert Fuoss.

Extended Run

"Let's hope you show well in the ratings," the television star told his son, as the boy presented his report card.

"Sorry, dad," replied the lad. "They want to sign me up to do another thirteen weeks this summer."

Out of Luck

A class of first graders were discussing brothers and sisters. "I don't have a sister," one little girl said wistfully.

Kids

"Just two brothers and the baby—and now the baby's turning into a boy, too."
—Lane Olinghouse.

Pay Raise

"I'm old enough to have my own place and live my own life," a daughter confidently announced to her parents. "The only problem," she added, "is that I'll need a bigger allowance."
—Robert Fuoss.

Beauty Spot

"Freckles would be a terrific suntan," sighed the teenaged girl, "if they'd only get together."

Daffynitions

Precocious baby: flash in the pram.
—Shelby Friedman.

Tantrums: Gripes of wrath.
—Raymond J. Cvikota.

Baby's first cry: inaugural bawl.
—Robert Fuoss.

Scullery-Duggery

Two children approached their mother in the kitchen and asked what she was making. When she told them the mixture in the bowl was plum pudding they asked, "But where are the plums?"

"Plums aren't used," answered the mother.

"Then why is it called plum pudding?"

Quickly, the older child replied, "Oh, that's its nom de plum!"
LaVada Weir.

Reprieve

"We're terribly sorry to be getting home so late," the father apologized to the weary baby-sitter.

"Don't worry about it," the battle-scarred girl replied. "If I were you, I wouldn't be in a hurry to get home either."

Self-Sufficiency?

An adolescent is a youngster who is old enough to dress himself if he could just remember where he dropped his clothes.

Game's Name

Adolescence is the age when boys discover girls—and girls discover they've been discovered.

Relief Note

The boy asked his father if he had any work he could do around the house to replenish his depleted finances. After giving the matter serious thought, the father admitted that he could think of nothing.

"Then," suggested the youngster, "how about putting me on welfare?"
—Herm Albright.

Bunny Hop

Delighted to receive two live baby rabbits for Easter, the youngster enjoyed them even more as they grew up. The mother and father, however, were getting anxious to dispose of the pets. One day the father asked, "Son, how would you like to have one of your rabbits for dinner tonight?"

The child's face brightened, "Sure, Daddy, but how would he hold his spoon?"

They kept the rabbits.

Next Question?

Eight-year-old Danny asked his father what the word "extinct" meant.

"Well," replied Dad after a moment's thought, "suppose that all of life on earth was wiped out, then you could say that the human race was extinct."

Danny pondered this explanation for a while, then queried, "But who would you say it to?"

Kids

Artful Dodgers
The kids know if they tell
    Mom's age
That they will get a scolding;
So their answer to the
    question now
Is: "She's thirty-nine, and
    holding."
                    —G. O. Ludcke.

Portrait of Innocence
I saw a baby
Just baptized.
He seemed so pure
And pastorized.
                    —Richard Armour.

Point of Departure
The moment you definitely
    know
That your children are
    growing
Is when they stop asking you
    where they came from—
And won't tell you where
    they're going.
                    —Gail Cooke.

Generation Gripe
A recent study indicates
that many teenagers are
opposed to sex education in
the schools. They say it's a
plot by parents and educators
to make the subject dull and
uninteresting.
                    —Edward Stevenson.

"You not only discriminate against me because I'm
a kid, but because I'm a woman!"

Kids

Independent Thinker

As the teen-ager took off for a party, his parents called after him, "Have a good time."

"Look, mom and pop," replied the rebel, "don't tell me what to do!"

Clean Start

He doesn't drink or smoke or
    swear,
He resists girls like a Spartan.
(Let's hope he'll continue the
    same life style
When he finishes
    kindergarten).
        —George O. Ludcke.

Bad Seed

It often happens that the apple of a parent's eye is the kid who's rotten to the core.
        —S. S. Biddle.

Parents

"Any instructions, or do I just wing it?"

Parents

Fine Art
Parenthood is the art of bringing up children without putting them down.
—Franklin P. Jones.

Grizzly Story
It was hardly long ago,
Yet his swings are now gone;
And his little bat and balls—
They, too, have moved on.

There stands the tricycle
On which he had such fun;
And our back yard is hushed,
Where he used to laugh and
    run.

It seems like only yesterday—
It is all so weird—
That our nice little boy
Is this boob with the beard!
—Arnold J. Zarett.

Recreational Note
An oldtimer is a parent who remembers back to the time when Creative Playthings were frogs, cigar boxes and mud puddles.
—Pru Pratt.

Changing Times
A father's lament: "When I was a boy, my dad told me to get out of the house and not to come back until I amounted to something— meaning, with a job. But now, my son refuses to leave until he finds a job with meaning!
        Marguerite Whitley May.

Boomerang!
One by one our children
    married
With the usual fuss—
And shortly after, two by two
They moved back in with us.
—Anna Herbert.

Spare the Child!
[*"Europeans are surprised at the deference shown to American children by parents." —News note.*]
We cradle and coddle our
    kids too long
And worry too much about
    them;
Instead of "giving them things
    we didn't have,"
They'd be better off without
    them.
—George O. Ludcke.

Sibling Revelry
"What's a house without
    children?"
Some folks are prone to ask.
And when by this query
I am taken to task,
A tempting reply is:
"I'd sure like to try it,
Because quite unlike ours,
It's bound to be quiet."
—Gail Cooke.

At Bat
Whenever my kids misbehave
It is I who feel bitter.
Because according to my wife
I'm the designated hitter.
—Arnold J. Zarett.

Mother Knows Best
A young woman was trying to decide whether or not to date a man several years her senior. "Do you think he's too old to be considered eligible?" she asked her mother, who was somewhat of a social climber.
Replied mama: "Darling, he's too eligible to be considered old!"
—Daisy Brown.

Smart Papa
"How do you get your son to rake leaves with such enthusiasm?" a man was asked by his neighbor. "He's been out there all afternoon!"
"I told him I dropped the car keys in the yard."
—Thomas Henry.

Truth Capsules
Those who really like children become teachers; those who don't often become parents.
—M. D. Reay.

Parents

Patience is what parents have when there are witnesses.
—Franklin P. Jones.

Over Bite
Though some folks play at
   poor-mouthing,
With me the sentiment's
   honest,
For I've just returned with the
   kids
From a trip to the
   orthodontist.
—Edward F. Dempsey.

Growing Pains
It costs a fortune to raise a family nowadays—but nothing to what you spend on them after they've grown up.
—Robert Fuoss.

Vox Pop?
Fathers who encourage their
   sons
To follow in their own
   footsteps are shaken
On such occasions as when
   they remember
Some of the steps they have
   taken.
—R. M. Walsh.

No Low Profile
Anybody who doubts that truth will out probably doesn't have children who talk to the neighbors.
—Franklin P. Jones.

Sorry, Dad
By the time you realize your father was right after all, your own son is old enough to disagree with you.
—Paul Harwitz.

Babes in Toyland
What are two signs
That make parents tremble?
"Batteries Not Included" and
"Easy to Assemble"!
—Gail Cooke.

Firm Treatment
The laying on of the hands
Can do wonders, it is said,
And my experience proves
We are not being misled.

It's not because it's relaxing
That I hold it in high regard,
But my kids behave so nicely
When I lay my hands on—
   hard.
—Arnold J. Zarett.

Choose One
"You've made your bed," the despairing mother told her slapdash teenage daughter, "and now you'll have to lie in it—although personally, I think you'll be a lot more comfortable on the floor!"
—Edward Stevenson.

Long Division
The generation gap really came apart when the carport succeeded the woodshed.
—Bill Copeland.

Daffynitions
Parent: Nix-Master.
—Jack Kraus.

Parents: forbearing animals.
—Robert Fitch.

Self-reliance: going off the depend.
—Raymond J. Cvikota.

Apparel Peril
A harried young woman, clad only in a suit jacket and slip, approached the Lost and Found Department in a huge department store and inquired frantically, "Has anybody turned in a black skirt with five children from two to six years old hanging on to it?"

Are You Listening, Daughter?
I don't like bangs that cover
   eyes,
I don't like skirts that
   challenge thighs,
I think that slacks should be
   well-fitting—
Not just for standing, but for
   sitting,

Parents

Eyeshadow's fine in blue or
    green—
But no, not for a girl
    thirteen.
And as for boys, their new
    long hair
Is unappealing. Call me
    square.
Your dances make me flip
    my lid—
And, no! I never was a kid!
                —Lyla Blake Ward.

Sour Loser
    The wedding ceremony was
in progress and the young
groom said, "With all my
worldly goods I thee endow."
    "Uh-oh," muttered his
father under his breath, "there
goes his ball-point pen!"
                —Anna Herbert.

Dubious Reward
    When the college girl
brought her latest romance
home to meet the folks, her
father boasted to the young
man, "The fellow who marries
my daughter is going to get
a prize!"
    "Is that so, sir?" asked the
boy, his eyes lighting up,
"And what is it?"

Teenager's Report
    If there's anything worse
than a parent who forgets

what it is to be young—it's
one who remembers.
                —Franklin P. Jones.

Growing Pains
Hearing their children's
    language
Has some parents in a daze
—
But mine, I like to think,
Are just going through a
    phrase.
                —Mimi Kay.

Note of Cheer
The good thing about having
your children home from
school: It takes your mind off
your other troubles.

Full Circle
If a parent will cling
To a truth that will bring
The strength to persist and
    endure,
He will find one day soon
Retribution is strewn
Where all of the obstacles
    were.
For a wise parent knows
When a little child grows
And gets to be tall and
    mature,
There are no past defenses
Or old insolences
That some kids of his own
    will not cure!
                —Alison Wyrley Birch.

Thank Goodness for Bees!
    [*"Drug-Coated Product Acts
as Oral Contraceptive,
Reduces Bird Population."*—
WSJ headline]
There goes another era!
Now how do we instill
The facts of life in children
When the birds are on the
    pill?
                —E. V. Girand.

Memo to Parents
Be kind to your kids
Through their sunny teens;
Remember where they got
Those funny genes!
                —L. Worth.

Eye Opener
    Two mothers were
discussing the difficulties of
getting their teenagers up and
out of the house in the
morning. The first one said "I
haven't had a bit of trouble
lately, however, I just open
his bedroom door and throw
the cat on his bed."
    "And that awakens your
son?" asked the second
woman incredulously.
    "It certainly does. He sleeps
with the dog."

Hush!
What is a home without
    children?
Really, the experts should try
    it.

Parents

They tell us it's lonely and
    barren,
But neglect to report that it's
    quiet.
             —Robert Fuoss.

Outdoor Payground
You know that summer
camp is going to be
expensive when it lists the
weenie roast as a "frankfurter
flambe."
             —Arch Napier.

Suggestion Box
Try a practical approach
next summer; send the dog
to camp and the kids to
obedience school.
             —Paul Harwitz.

Candid Comments
Consenting adults have
been with us for a long time,
and they are mostly parents.
             —Bert H. Kruse.

Children will usually obey if
you explain patiently what
you want them to do—and
stand over them while they
do it.
             —Franklin P. Jones.

Disciplinary Note
Knowing her father to be a
pushover, the teenaged girl
demanded an increase in her

"Just put the quarter under his pillow, Harry."

Parents

allowance. Replied dad: "I'm not giving you another penny, and that's semi-final."
—D. B. Brown.

Articulation
Though the accent might be
    on youth,
It should be quite apparent
That the stress is actually
    placed
Invariably upon the parent!
—Ruth M. Walsh.

Final Analysis
Some parents have rigid rules,
While others are permissive;
Some parents will not give in,
While others are submissive.

Opinions differ on whether
To come on gentle or strong,
But in the end all agree:
Whatever they did was wrong.
—Arnold J. Zarett.

Speed Rearing
Children are a great comfort in your old age, and they help you get there faster, too.
—H. E. Martz.

The Gap Trap
The Lord made parents a bit
    too old
To tell their kids what they
    should be told.
Twenty-five years with no
overlap
Is the length of the
    generation gap.
So any advice from a Dad or
    Mother
Goes in one era and out the
    other.
—Alison Wyrley Birch.

Unfinished Business
Back around the turn of the century, psychologists taught us that children are complex beings in their own right, not merely miniature adults. What we need now is someone to explain to the kids that we adults are people, too—not just enlarged children.
—Martha C. Brown.

Car Pall
In our suburban area
Life is a carpool existence,
Since everywhere kids must
    go
Is not within walking distance.
So you can readily
    understand why,
It's just a matter of course,
Dad is head of the household
But Mom is the driving force
—Cobby Ellen Falkoff.

Super Squelch
Upon receiving a report from a nursery school that her daughter was emotionally immature, a mother sent the school this reply: "If you can't be immature at three, when can you be?"
—Harold Helfer.

Recital Pay-off
I've sat through songs sung
    out of key,
Through violins played
    screechily,
Through torturings of the bass
    fiddle,
Guitar chords forgotten in the
    middle,
And my reward is on the
    way:
It's finally my kid's turn to
    play.
—Donna Evleth.

Marital Mixups

"As a last resort, would you two consider a week's summit at Camp David?"

Identity Crisis

There are two types of
    people (so say the reports):
One loves opera; the other
    loves sports;
One loves the mountains; the
    other, the ocean;
One wants to relax; the other
    craves motion;
One prefers silence each
    morning—no matter!
The other one thrives on a
    morning of chatter:
And what causes them so
    much struggle and strife?
They always end up as
    husband and wife!
                    —Gloria Rosenthal.

Civil Rites

In a simple, civil service
The couple's knot was tied,
The groom was pale and
nervous,
As was his pretty bride.
Their honeymoon was harried,
Their wedded life grew tense;
Although they are still
    married,
They've not been civil since.
                    —Ellie Womack.

Patched Up

Another quarrel has cleared
    the air,
But our marriage is not in
    clover;
It seems whenever we make
    our peace

Marital Mixups

There are a few scraps left
over.
—Thomas Usk.

The Mating Game
A sure prelude to
A domestic uproar
Is a dozen mixed socks
In a dark bureau drawer.
—G. Sterling Leiby.

Sign of the Times
My wife and I rarely converse
But I have no trepidation.
Either I'm out playing tennis,
Or she's deep in meditation.
—Arnold J. Zarett.

Wry Words
A marital battle
Can be quite a bruiser;
The winner will often
Feel worse than the loser.
—Elinor K. Rose.

Daffynition
Marriage counselor's office:
travail bureau.

Dentifrice Destiny
Some are roll-the-bottom kind,
And some are squeeze-the-
middle kind.
Why is it every former kind
Gets married to a latter kind?
—Ramona Demery.

Spectacles
What couples see in one
another
Sometimes makes you
wonder, brother!
You think you maybe should
insist
They get a new optometrist,
Until you wonder if their view
May be the same as yours
and you!
—Bert Kruse.

Incompatible
My vision is myopic,
But at forty-plus I see
Very, very clearly things
I hold in front of me.

But at a distance eyesight
lags,
While he who is my mate,
Sees perfectly for miles away,
But not what's on his plate.

So at the crossroads here we
stand
Unable now to try,
Despite our years of married
life,
To see things eye to eye.
—Alison Wyrley Birch.

Sweet Reasonableness
That I'm scoring a point
Is abundantly clear
When my spouse murmurs
sweetly,
"Let's not argue, my dear."
—Rebecca Wilde.

Trying the Knot
These days, it seems, we wed
a lot;
And ditto for divorce.
Although we flunk as like as
not
We just repeat the course.
So are we happier now we
Have leapt the wedlock
barrier?
Well, happier we may not be—
But certainly we're marrier!
—G. Sterling Leiby.

Divorce

"You say he siphoned the gas from your car into his car. Yes, I think that would be grounds for divorce."

Altar Rations

A fellow confessed to his
  friend,
"I got married to escape
From going to the laundromat
And wearing socks with holes
  agape.
I was tired of frozen dinners,
Tending garden in season—"
"That's funny," interrupted the
  friend,
"I got divorced for the same
  reason."

—R. M. Walsh.

Pair-anoia

Some couples get
The urge
To merge,
While others get
A writ
To split.

—G. Sterling Leiby.

Honeymoon Tune

The divorce rate would go
  down
If couples understood
That instead of marrying for
  better or worse,
They should just marry for
  good.

—Ruth M. Walsh.

Freedom Fighters

Divorce means
Something different to
Each set it's found among:
Some think

Divorce

They've been deserted,
And others, that they've been
    sprung.
                    —E. B. de Vito.

Daffynitions
    Divorce: ending up loose
ties.
                    —Len Elliott.

    Divorce: connubial blitz.

    Divorce: Buss stop.
                    —Raymond J. Cvikota.

Candid Comment
    The rocketing divorce rate
suggests that marriage is what
keeps many women occupied
while they wait for the right
man to come along.
                    —Franklin P. Jones.

Domesticated

Who, Him?
Hometown is the place where
    you were born
And then grew up as a kid
(And where everyone
    wonders, when you return
How you turned out as well
    as you did.)
                    —George O. Ludcke.

Domestic Note
    Perhaps the greatest
housekeeping aid these days
is a television set that doesn't
work.
                    —Franklin P. Jones.

My Sugar's Coating
My wife wants to buy a fur
    coat,
But I tell her not to be rash.
"Save the poor animals,
    dear," I say,
But I think to myself, "Save
    my cash."
                    —Richard Armour.

Hangups
In closets and in vestibules
Where scads of hangers
    dangle
I reach with care for one
    alone
But always get a tangle.
                    —Bert Kruse.

Test Palate
    The young bride had put
up a valiant struggle to learn
how to cook. Her devoted
husband suffered through her
numerous culinary goofs with
a smile and no-comments
policy. It was only after he'd
asked her to bake him a
cake that the real crisis
occurred.
    Greeting him that evening
in tears, she cried, "I made
the cake you asked for. But
the dog ate it!"
    "Please, darling, don't cry,"
soothed her husband. I'll buy
you another dog."

Dress Rehearsal
My wife is trying on a dress.
I stand by for advice.
She asks me, "Darling, how's
    the fit?"
I ask her, "What's the price?"
                    —Richard Armour.

Daffynition
    Moving day: Hearth
transplant.
                    —Raymond J. Cvikota.

Basics
    The surest way to get
down to the real nitty-gritty is
to eat lunch on the beach.
                    —Gertrude Pierson.

She Cared!
Lot's wife looked back, and
    turned to salt,
Which wasn't really Lot's

Domesticated

"Well—your clothesline is good and tight now."

wife's fault.
To punish her was most
   unkind;
She only thought she'd left a
   lot behind!
                    —Ann R. Franco.

Birthday Party for Mom
We give her the gifts,
We wish her best wishes,
We serve her the cake—
Then she does the dishes.
                    —William T. Hogan.

Speed Checked
   A male shopper in the
supermarket stood at the
counter looking at the bill
he'd just been handed.
   "That sure was fast," he
remarked to the checkout
clerk. "How many dollars a
minute can you tape?"
                    —Walter Anthony.

False Alarm
   "When you discovered that
all the dresser drawers had
been ransacked," said the
investigator, "why didn't you
phone the police
immediately?"
   "Well," the woman replied,
"I thought at first my
husband had been looking for
a clean shirt."
                    —Paul Harwitz.

Domesticated

Shout From the Shower
You who phone me, please
    hang on there.
One more ring and I'd have
    been there!
        —Richard Armour.

Guilty on All Counts
"Henry," the young wife
announced to her husband, "I
just found a letter in a
woman's handwriting in the
pocket of your brown suit."

"In my pocket?" the
mystified husband cried, "Why,
I swear I don't know how it
got there!"

"Well, I do," replied his
wife calmly. "I wrote it and
gave it to you to mail two
weeks ago."
        —F. G. Kernan.

Liquid Asset
At this time of the year
All those big bills I fear,
Run up by my wife and my
    daughter.
So, to prevent them I try,
Saying, "The well has run
    dry,"
But to them it doesn't hold
    water.
        —Leonard Dittell.

No Press Release
Shirts and trousers are
    acclaimed
As permanently pressed.

And science now takes quite
    a bow,
But may I please suggest
That though I'm just a simple
    sort
And get no praise or cheers,
By job and wife and sundry
    strife
I've been hard pressed for
    years.
        —Richard Armour.

Rest Rumor
Ten hours of sleep are
    required by some,
Others get by on four;
But when the alarm goes off,
    we all
Need just five minutes more.
        —G. O. Ludcke.

Words From Their Wives
Mrs. Edison: "Must you
make light of everything?"

Mrs. Washington: "I wish
you didn't think you had to
be first at everything!"

Mrs. Fulton: "Now what are
you so steamed up about?"
        —George M. Dodson.

First Things First
A distraught woman rushed
into a drugstore. Interrupting
the druggist, who was busy
with another customer, she
cried, "This is an emergency!
My husband was painting the
house and the ladder slipped

out from under him. He's
hanging to the roof by his
hands."

"So you'll be needing first-
aid supplies?"

"That can wait," the
woman panted. "What I want
right now is a roll of film for
my camera!"
        —Pru Pratt.

Gold Mine
"I don't think our town
would support a canine
obedience school," the local
banker told the businessman
who sought his advice. "But
if you really want to make a
bundle, and aren't afraid to
take on kids . . .!"
        —Edward Stevenson.

Offsprings' Off Season
Time was when families were
    large,
I scarce knew one that
    wasn't;
But now young marrieds use
    restraint—
It's cheaper by the doesn't.
        —Dick Emmons.

All About Eden
Adam and Eve had an ideal
    marriage.
He didn't have to hear about
    the men she could have
    wed.

Domesticated

And she, in turn, didn't have
   to hear about
The way his mother cooked
   and baked bread.
       —Ruth M. Walsh.

Sweet Smell of Success
My culinary efforts
Would never win a prize.
My housekeeping is so-so,
I'm not witty or wise.

Yet my husband brings
   flowers,
He whistles all day long.
I am doing something right—
Or he's done something
   wrong.
       —Gail Cooke.

Passe Models
The Smiths are strange;
Their contentment waxes.
They like their lives,
They pay their taxes.
They're quite happy
With what they'e got—
They'll never make
A TV plot.
       —Robert Gordon.

Daffynitions
   A mother's recollections:
Momoir..
       —Dutch Cohen.

   Moving day: Hearth
transplant.
       —Raymond J. Cvikota.

   Snoring: sheet music.
       —Herm Albright.

   Sewing circle: frock group.
       —Len Elliott.

   Family get-together: sibling
revelry.
       —Francis E. Butler.

   Fear of confrontation: the
qualm before the storm.
       —Pam Cascioli.

True Paradise
In or out of the Garden,
Adam and Eve had it made,
They could frolic in innocent
   pleasure,
Then rest in a snug little
   glade.

They could eat when their
   bellies felt empty;
Whey dry, they could hoist
   up a drink,
And never once have to
   consider
"What will the neighbors
   think?"
       —Jo Anne Hoffman
          Johnson.

Matching Game
My wife hands me a
   shopping list
And I go to the store
   undaunted.

Knowing that when I return
She'll say: "That's not what I
   wanted."
       —Arnold J. Zarett.

Candid Comment
   Sentimentalists are wont to
inquire, "What is a home
without children?" Well, if
they're listening, the answer is:
quiet!
       —Robert Fuoss.

At a Loss
There's hardly an hour of the
   day that passes
Without my inquiring, "Where
   are my glasses?"
Though now and then, just
   for a change of pace,
I ask, "Have you seen my
   glasses case?"
       —Richard Armour.

Education

"Read me my report card, Dad."

Fat Chance
I never miss class reunions,
My support for them is
    staunch;
For I long to meet old
    classmates
Who've beaten me to the
    paunch.
            —Edward F. Dempsey.

Transported
One thing that always has me
    fussing
Is "busing" that is written
    "bussing."
It's not misspelled—the
    spelling varies,
And both are in most
    dictionaries.
But buss, not bus, you know
    means kiss.
And bussing thus may be
    amiss,
Unless, of course, the bussing
    students
Who have no shame and
    have no prudence,
Unknown to parents, as a
    rule
Both bus and buss their way
    to school.
            —Richard Armour.

Drag Race
Many students don't read
    well,
But this problem they can
    master;
By taking speed reading
    courses

Education

They can read poorly much
    faster.
                        —Arnold J. Zarett.

Up and Out
Graduation is a thrill
That's double, in a way.
Your children graduate from
    school
And you from PTA.
                    —Richard Armour.

Bad News
"Your child is inattentive,
insolent and disruptive in
class," the teacher complained
to a parent. "But that's the
least of my problems. He has
a perfect attendance record!"
                    —Bess Beavers.

Classified Entreaty
Ad in a college newspaper:
"Female, 45, desires to
correspond with male student,
19; her son."
                    —Lane Olinghouse.

Note of Concern
"Dear dad," said the letter
from the university, "I haven't
heard from you in a month.
Why don't you drop me a
check to let me know you're
okay?"
                    —Lane Olinghouse.

Daffynitions
Diploma: remembrance of
things passed.
                    —Honey Greer.

Thesis time: writes of spring.
                    —Antoni Tabak.

Planetarium: Eclipse Joint.
                    —Jack Kraus.

Rest period: niche of time.
                    —Len Elliott.

Girl Scout banquet: The lass
supper.
                    —Raymond J. Cvikota.

Education Updated
A doctor, attending the 50th
reunion of his graduating
class, was asked his opinion
of his old alma mater.
"I'm disappointed in one
thing," he replied. "I sat in
on some of the final exams
and discovered that you're
still asking the same questions
you had on the exams when
I was in school."
"That's right," said one school
official. "But today we're
getting some new answers."
                    —Herm Albright.

Little Big Men
Two very callow college
freshmen slid into a booth at

the campus hangout. "Is
anyone looking at us?"
whispered the first boy.
"Not that I can see."
"Good! We won't have to
order a beer!"
                    —Daisy Brown.

Labor Problem
Today's children seem to be
born with two strikes against
them: teachers and school bus
drivers.
                    —Robert Fuoss.

Credited Course
A fourth grade teacher was
trying to impress upon her
students the importance of
penmanship. "If you can't
write your name, when you
grow up you'll have to pay
cash for everything."
                    —Paul Harwitz.

Low Grade Infection
When it comes to college,
I'm losing my patience
At courses they label
"Communications."
I wouldn't be scornful,
Their catalogues slighting,
If only they'd teach the kids
Reading and writing.
                    —Robert Gordon.

New Math
In sprawling southern
California, it's reported that

Education

suburban schools teach addition, subtraction, multiplication—and subdivision!
—Robert Fuoss.

Lot to Learn
Overheard at a PTA meeting, one teacher to another: "I prefer to teach in an elementary school—I know I'll have a place to park my car."

Educational Benefits
Poster on the bus shows an unhappy lad over this caption: "Don't be like me. I were a school drop-out."
Some wag scribbled underneath; "Not me. I goed on to college."

Entrance Exam
Nowadays, when a boy is accepted by a college he can't tell whether they liked his test scores or his father's credit rating.
—Robert Fuoss.

Short Thrift
In outfitting her son for his first year of prep school, a mother hoped to cut costs by shopping in a big store's bargain basement. After carefully studying a heap of shirts on a table, she turned to her shopping companion and said, "These shirts are a bargain, but they're all monogrammed and I can't find one with a "J" for Johnny!"
"Listen," said her friend,! "for eighty-nine cents you can give him a nickname for the school term!"
—Anna Herbert.

Stumper
The boy approached his father about a homework problem. "Dad, I have to bring to the class tomorrow a simple explanation of 'inflation' and also of Einstein's theory of relativity. Can you help me?"
"Okay, son," his dad replied. "Suppose we begin with the easiest—Einstein's theory."
—Herm Albright.

Truth Capsule
The fellow driving fastest past a school was perhaps the slowest getting through it.
—Arnold Glasow.

School Note
Effective education was when the students were driven in school and not to.
—Raymond J. Cvikota.

Kid Stuff
The best you can say for most day care nurseries is that they fill a crying need.
—Robert Fuoss.

Modern Version
There's a child psychologist
who claims,
Of the kids he treats these
days,
That he can't remember all
their names,
But he never forgets a phase.
—S. S. Biddle.

Hang-up
Home front objections
To sex education
In schools are quite likely to
show
That parents are fearful
Their children may learn
The things that they already
know.
—E. B. de Vito.

Example
On learning that his son was stealing pencils from school, a horrified father summoned the boy for a stern lecture. He started out by saying, "You don't have to do that. You know I bring home plenty from the office!"

Education

Natural Likeness

A father and son were posing for a picture at the time of the young man's graduation from college.

"Stand a bit closer to your father," said the photographer to the graduate, "and put your hand on his shoulder."

"Wouldn't it be more appropriate," said the father, "if he stood with his hand in my pocket?"

—F. G. Kernan.

Question Marked

Inquisitive tots
Receive no replies—
I have run out of
Words to the why's.

—Gail Cooke.

The Old Math

The most successful way to teach your children to count is to give them different allowances.

—Paul Harwitz.

Housekeeping

"Not *that* kind of a leak. A LEAK leak!"

Housekeeping

Earth Mother
Barefoot I stand
In sifted sand.
Upon the shore?
No, bathroom floor!
—Nova Trimble Ashley.

Lost in the Backwash
Among the unsolved riddles
　of life
For pundits to ponder on
Is, why—after socks are
　laundered—
One of each pair is gone.
　—George O. Ludcke.

The Privileged's Information
I always used to fix the sink
Whenever it went on the
　blink,
And would repair the wiring
With great effort and
　perspiring,
And do the painting and
　plastering, too,
Just like the other amateurs
　do.
But all these labors I now
　shun
Since I can afford to have
　them done
By professionals who,
　curiously,
Perform them most
　amateurishly.
　—Leonard Dittell.

Royal Rip-off
That our home is our castle
Is a term with which we're all
acquainted;
But it really comes across
　when
We have an estimate to have
　it painted.
　—R. M. Walsh.

Social Study
A guest towel is usually
what makes you wonder how
your guests dried their hands.
　—Franklin P. Jones.

Decorating, Period
Most of our friends have
　strived for years
For homes that are unique.
They go for French provincial,
The modern or antique.
Our home cries out with
　atmosphere—
It takes imagination
To figure out what we've
　acquired—
It's called "conglomeration."
　—Naomi Gay.

When a House Becomes a Home
This lovely, unpretentious
　house:
Did I once call it cramped
　and small?
This pretty, winding corridor,
Did I once call a crooked
　hall?
This kitchen that I once
　disdained
Much pleasure now to me
　affords.
Where were my eyes when I
　dismissed
These fine old floors as
　creaking boards?
My long-held views and tastes
　have changed,
Far more, I find, than I can
　tell,
Between the time I bought
　my house
And then decided I must sell.
　—Lester A. Sobel.

Household Mystery
The ball-points that seem to
　have blossomed
All over the place
Can vanish when needed and
　leave not so much
As a trace.
Whatever the fate of these
　myriad pens that have fled,
Why couldn't it happen to
　wire coat-hangers instead?
　—Jane Herald.

Deduction
The haughty matron
inspected her living room and
declared to the cleaning lady:
"Phyllis, I see a spider web in
the corner. To what do you
attribute that?"
"Well, madam," the girl
replied, "I'd say to a spider."
　—Duane Dewlap.

Housekeeping

Gift Suggestion
A woman who's married to
a man who has everything
says she wishes someone
would give him something
that would pick it all up and
put it where it belongs.
—Edward Stevenson.

The Whirl Around Us
Another law of nature
Has become crystal clear:
While coat hangers multiply,
Ballpoint pens disappear.
—Gail Cooke.

Trash Compactor
It's just the device
For a trashy deposit;
We've had one for years—
We call it a closet.
—Ramona Demery.

To Each His Zone
When the homeowner
heard the price of cleaning
his chimneys, he snorted,
"Forget it! I'll clean them
myself!"
"Okay," shrugged the
chimneysweep, "soot yourself."
—Edward Stevenson.

Basic Boot
When household things
Get out of whack
And won't be fixed
With tool or tack,
They're often acting

Mean or fickle—
When work won't cure,
Perhaps a kick'll!
—Elinor K. Rose.

Daffynitions
Home repairs; the power of
positive tinkering.
—Raymond J. Cvikota.

Chaise longue: yawn
furniture..

Fire insurance: singe
benefits.
—Bess Beavers.

Fireplace repair: open
hearth surgery.
—Charles H. Chernov.

Unrepaired roof: swinging
shingles.
—Thomas Henry.

First Come, First Served
One benefit of the untidy
house
Is how burglars react;
They leave right after
entering, thinking
It's already been ransacked.
—George O. Ludcke.

Wood Butcher
I've a plumb line and a level,
A chisel, plane and bevel;

There is no job I will not try
to master,
I've an awfully classy mitre
And my drill bit is a biter—
But when I try to use them,
it's disaster.
—Leonard A. Paris.

Home Sweet Home
Maintenance costs more;
mortgages are higher;
Fuel and taxes amount to a
passel!
Verily, I say unto thee,
A man's home is his hassle!
—R. M. Walsh.

Sticky Problem
A drawer in the cabinet
sticks,
And would you believe my
luck—
The tool that I need to fix it
Is the thing in the drawer
that's stuck!
—Julia C. Ardayne.

What's Cooking?

"It says, 'place in micro wave oven for two minutes, basting every five seconds'."

COCHRAN!

Cold Fact

A recent safety survey shows that burns are no longer the most common kitchen accident. Now, it's frostbite.

—Robert Fuoss.

Daffynitions

Meat counter theft: Choplifting.

—Ralph Noel.

Barbecue chef: gratekeeper.
Pasta: noodlework.

—Daisy Brown.

Appetizer store in Tibet: the Deli Lama.

—Bernice P. Weiss.

Flaming dessert: A flash in the pan.

—June Brady.

Dinner Belle

Although her fried foods
  often grieve me.
To tell her off is not my
  plan.
You see, I'd miss her if she'd
  leave me:
I've grown accustomed to her
  pan.

— G. Sterling Leiby.

What's Cooking?

Parties

Report From the Cellar

The wine we serve's not
  smooth as silk,
Like chateau stuff or
  Liebfraumilch.
It comes from grapes we
  bought and tramped,
Fermented, bottled, corked
  and stamped.
We sip it fast (one could get
  loaded)
Before the rest of it's
  exploded!
                    —Bert Kruse.

Dining Doubts

Did I not know my wife's
  ragout
Is Boeuf-au-something, Cordon
  Bleu—
I'd swear that I am eating
  stew.
                    —F. R. Canning.

"It's your babysitter. She can't find the liquor."

Parties

Formal Complaint
I hate to dress formal!
To shave and be kempt!
I prefer an existence
That's tux exempt!
— Shelby Friedman.

No Party Pooper
Saturday night, I stoutly
  decree,
I'll spend at home in
  tranquility.
I want no part of any wild
  spree—
(Unless, of couse, someone
  invites me.)
— Arnold J. Zarett.

Sobering Thought
You never realize, until you
get cornered at a party by
some crashing bore, how
many things you're really not
interested in.
— Edward Stevenson.

Tolerance Tester
Throughout the party, a
loud-mouthed guest worked at
being the center of attention.
Later, the hostess said to her
husband, "I suppose we
should forgive him. He's
going through a nonentity
crisis."
— Robert Orben.

Party Platform
The life of the party
Is noisy and hearty.

I suffer whenever I see one.
It's hard to ignore him
When others adore him.
So I suffer—wanting to be
  one.
— Irene Warsaw..

Daffynitions
Cocktail party waiter:
boretender.
— Bess Beavers.

Cocktail party hostess: Din
mother.
— Raymond J. Cvikota.

Gate-crashers: nixed
company.
Lawn party hostess: Grass
hopper.
— Pru Pratt.

Party Language
The host who asks, "What's
  your hurry?"
Means it, I've come to know,
Just about as much as the
  guest
Who says, "I ought to go."
— Gail Cooke.

Party Primper
Go as I am?
Perish the thought!
Give me a moment
To go as I'm not.
— Nova Trimble Ashley.

Social Problem
Some folks like cocktail
  parties,
Where small talk is the rule—
Small talk is fine, but friends
  of mine
Make talk that's minuscule.
— Dick Emmons.

Exit Line
At five p.m. a woman said
to her maid, "Oh, by the
way, Nellie, my husband's
bringing four extra guests
home for dinner. Are you
prepared?"
"Not quite," replied the
maid. "But it never takes me
long to pack."
— Pru Pratt.

II THE HEALTHY LIFE

"How long have you been feeling as weak
as a dollar?"

Keeping Fit

"Open wide and say 'nevermore'."

Eye Opener
Our nation's hospital care
Is, without doubt, the finest—
    still,
Where else would you be
    awakened
To be given a sleeping pill?
    —Arnold J. Zarett.

Cold Bugged
The cold is doomed to
    vanish, like
The dodo and the bison,
Thanks to the aid of pills
    and sprays
And shots of streptomycin.

No more will vengeful viruses
Invade our solar plexus.
Though chances are, some
    tougher strain
Of bug will rise to vex us.
    —Edith Ogutsch.

Proof Negative
Our guests have gone, and
    no one smoked!
So odd, I really doubt it.
I look around. There are no
    ifs
Or ands or butts about it.
    —Richard Armour.

Conversation Peace
So you ask me how things
    are!
Should I mention my surgical
    scar,
My trick knee that's out of
    whack,

Keeping Fit

The root canal or sacroiliac,
My allergy, recurrent sneezes,
My sinusitis or migraine bout,
The flaming joint with acute
    gout,
My stolen car, business
    doldrums,
Or sticky little family
    problems?
So you want to know what's
    new!
Everything's fine, thanks. And
    you?
                    —Arnold J. Zarett.

Putdown

    Glaring angrily at the
young doctor, an elderly lady
patient snapped, "Don't you
dare tell me I'm all right,
young man! I was in failing
health before you were born."
                —Daphne Bettwing.

Gag Rule

While dental work for some
    is painful,
And frequently induces
    squawking,
My complaint is somewhat
    different—
It means I have to give up
    talking!
            —Rosemarie Williamson.

Health Care

    One advantage of the
ever-spiraling cost of medical
treatment is that it's cured a
lot of hypochondria.
                    —Paul Harwitz.

Vocal Yokel

Laryngitis isn't fatal,
Or so at least I hear.
Besides, I have it only once,
Yes, only once a year.

And I can tell when it will
    be,
Right to the very day:
It's when I have to make a
    speech
And cannot say my say.
                —Richard Armour.

Inhale and Hearty

    A man who hates physical
exertion was advised by his
doctor not to stop smoking.
After all, hacking and
coughing are the only
exercise he gets!
                —Bill Copeland.

The Killing Cure

I've found that some of the
    pills
I must take to treat my ills
May leave me feeling queasy,
Dizzy, sick and uneasy;
And where the doc gives me
    a shot
May turn into a painful knot;
Often I'd prefer to endure
My illness than to take its
    cure.
            —Colleen Stanley Bare.

Cold War

Why do we say we've caught
    a cold
When that is error manifold?
We do not cast with hook
    and lines,
Nor track it through the
    wood by signs.
Nor do we hunt it with a
    gun
Or overtake it on the run.
So when you sound your
    next kachoo,
Remember that a cold caught
    you!
                —Lance Oneal.

Facing Facts

I don't take beauty naps
And my reason is terse:
Whenever I get up
I always look worse.
                —Mimi Kay.

It Pours the Same

No pharmacopoeia has ever
    discussed
A mystery as old as the
    Druids:
It's liquids we drink when our
    health is robust,
But as soon as we're ailing
    it's fluids.
                —Norman Lowe.

Recovery Room

    "When am I going to get
out of the hospital?" surgical

Keeping Fit

patient anxiously asked the doctor.

"Don't worry," replied the medico. "You're going home the minute you're strong enough to face the cashier."
—Robert Fuoss.

Ups and Downs
Want to get exercise?
I'll tell you a sure-fire way:
Just sit in an aisle seat
At a children's matinee.
—Herm Albright.

No Winning
You can't win. We used to talk out our problems over cigarets and coffee—now they are the problems.
—H. E. Martz.

Too Late
The trouble with jogging is that by the time you realize you're in no condition for it, you've got a long walk to get back.
—Franklin P. Jones.

Group Therapy
When some small illness picks on me
And won't respond to medication,
There's one unfailing remedy:
A sudden party invitation.
—Irene Warsaw.

Hospital Gown
A scratch-type garment
Resembling a sack,
Designed by some varmint
To tie in the back.
It's too hot for sleeping,
It's homely as Ned,
But useful for keeping
The patient in bed.
—Betty Billipp.

Cautious
"Of course I have a number of doctors," the hypochondriac snapped. "You don't catch me putting all my aches in one basket."
—Edward Stevenson.

Life Lines
Psychiatrists' couches would empty
If more patients learned this equation:
Happiness is a way of traveling—
And not a destination.
—G. O. Ludcke.

Daffynitions
Severe case of hives: an embarrassment of itches.
—Jane Otten.

Neurotic: one who is beset in his ways.
—Shelby Friedman.

Head cold: rheum at the top.
—Robert Fitch.

Headache: Temple tantrum.
—Dana Robbins.

Anesthetist: numb dropper.
—Pru Pratt.

Daily exercises: a battle of the flexes.
Neurotic: in a clash by himself.
—Shelby Friedman.

That's Life Dept.
Some people never look up until they are flat on their backs.
—H. E. Martz.

Intensive Prayer
I ordered nurses 'round the clock,
But what I should have said
Was: "Do not stay around the clock—
Please stay around the bed!"
—Gloria Rosenthal.

Convalescent's Complaint
"I can understand the $250 per day for the semi-private room," the discharged patient said, as he went over his bill with the hospital's

Keeping Fit

credit department. "And I can understand the dollar apiece for aspirin and the fifty cents a glass for drinking water. But what's this five-hundred dollar initiation fee?"
—Edward Stevenson.

Jaws
Brush each day,
Of sweets stay clear,
See your dentist
Twice a year.
For I have ventured
(In fact, maintained)
That nothing dentured,
Nothing pained.
—Dow Richardson.

Medi-Card
We should all work at staying well these days. Aside from rising medical costs, have you priced Get-Well Cards?
—Gil Stern.

Sty Ways
"Swine Flu Inoculation Schedule Reaches Half-way Mark."—News Item.]
The population is now half-shot
While pundits still pro and con it;
Some regard it as a pig-in-a-poke—
While others go whole hog on it.
—George O. Ludcke.

Shopper's Guide
[*"Hospitals adopt marketing tactics to promote services. ." WSJ news item.*]
Tell me about your food,
Your labs and decor,
And how many nurses
Are found on each floor.

Who are your doctors,
Describe their schools;
Let's see your list
Of diagnostic tools.

I hope you don't think
I'm being too quizzical;
I'd like a nice buy
On a good physical.
—Arnold J. Zarett.

Post-Op
They get you out of bed so fast,
I fear they'll soon be prone
To send you back from surgery
Upright, and on your own!
—Gloria Rosenthal.

Blood Reckoning
When they take blood for blood tests,
There's one fact I deplore:
They always take it when I'm sick
And couldn't need it more!
—Donna Evleth.

Projected Sylph Esteem
I'm going to jog three miles each day,

I'm going to take up tennis;
I'm going to think of exercise
As fun, and not a menace.
I'm going to buy a trampoline,
I'm going to stand up straighter;
I'm going to get in perfect shape,
I really am—but later.
—Mary-Gene Marr.

Security Blanket
[*"Stored leftover swine flu vaccine may remain effective for ten years".—WSJ news item.*]
Regarding the swine flu,
We need have no cares;
Enough vaccine's stored
For a decade of scares.
—Arnold J. Zarett.

Medical Risk
If I catch a disease
I can get cured for,
I hope it's something
That I'm insured for.
—Robert Gordon.

Needle Shy
Consider the sting of the porcupine's quill,
Hold on to the thought and combine, if you will
With instant revulsion on seeing a snake
To help comprehend the position I take

Keeping Fit

That never, at any
   conceivable juncture
Could I be persuaded to try
   acupuncture!
                    —Jane Herald.

Common Cold Mystery
   Why is it that the merest
titter of a sneeze will get you
"God bless you's" and
"Gesundheits" by the score;
but when you almost cough
yourself to death, all you get
are dirty looks?
                    —Edward Stevenson.

Test Case
   These days a wonder
drug is one that has no
effect on mice.
                    —Gil Stern.

Reformer
Willpower's something that,
   when
It's working,
You quit smoking and start
   smirking.
                    —Suzanne Douglass.

Dialogue Dilemma
Talk out your problems,
Psychologists stress.
But this method, with me,
Hasn't met with success.
I find it conflicts
With one other tip:

I can't talk while keeping
A stiff upper lip.
                    —Arnold J. Zarett.

Menace
   Perhaps nothing's more
dangerous to the human race
than the nuclear bomb, the
laser beam and the forgotten
roller skate.
                    —Franklin P. Jones.

Stress

Hemographics
You can take your own
   blood pressure
In a franchised booth in
   stores
And chart your hypertension
As the cost of living soars.
                    —Raymond Leary.

Low Blow
The truest frustration
Is when you live with stress—
Find you have an ulcer
And still aren't a success.
                    —Gail Cooke.

Whim and Vigor
Cheerful people are the ones
   who may
Resist disease, so doctors say.
In other words, some medics
   affirm—
The surly bird catches the
   germ.
                    —Gail Cooke.

Bitter Medicine
   ["Sixteen Million
Americans Each Consume
Two Pounds or More of
Tranquilizers Annually."—News
headline.]
I know that we live in a pill-
   popping age
But sometimes the headlines
   ring hollow:
"Two pounds of pills per
   annum"?

Stress

I find that a bit hard to
    swallow!
           —G. O. Ludcke.

Motivation Query
So many millions of
Americans are on tranquilizers
these days, one wonders what
the country's calming to.
           —Shelby Friedman.

Qualms About Calming
While in theory it should
    work,
This doesn't jibe with facts;
Since you just get more
    uptight
When someone says: "Relax!"
         —Rosemarie Williamson.

Daffynition
Nervous wreck: one who's
in perpetual emotion.
         —Robert Fuoss.

Distress Signal
I ought to give up worrying,
Yes, I really ought.
If what I fear will happen,
    doesn't,
The worrying's been for
    naught;
If what I fear will happen,
    does,
The worrying's been in vain,
For when it happens I will
    just
Be worrying again.

"Phillip, I wish you wouldn't take your
relaxation so hard."

Stress

Makes sense—so now I'm all
     a-flurry
Worrying how to get rid of
     worry.
                    —A. S. Flaumenhaft.

Cover Story
Though at times I may feel
     tense
My face will never show it;
The inner turmoil's there,
But those around don't know
     it.

I appear a picture of strength,
Of this there is no doubt;
But that's not the way I'd
     look
If I were inside out.
                    —Arnold J. Zarett.

Ill at Ease
Combating stress adds years
     to your life,
Of this there's no denying;
But often in getting rid of it,
I get tensed up from trying.
                    —Edward F. Dempsey.

Painfully Unfair
Success and ulcers go
     together,
Most doctors are agreed.
Two years ago I got an ulcer —
How come I don't succeed?
                    —William Lodge.

Middle Aged
     [*"Man's average life
expectancy was 47 years at
the turn of the century."—
News note*]
I'm not so sure that the
     Good Old Days
Were the best time to be
     alive,
When Middle-Age Anxiety
Started at age twenty-five.
                    —George O. Ludcke.

Lesson in Calm
When things go wrong most
     folks are prone
To make a big production.
They clutch their heads and
     moan and groan—
They need expert instruction.

They're fools to yelp so
     raucously
With punctuating wails.
Why don't they just relax like
     me
And bite their fingernails?
                    —Georgie Starbuck Galbraith

Fun Fearful
     A woman went to Europe
for the first time. After several
busy weeks in touring the
continent, she wired her
psychiatrist: "Having Wonderful
Time. Why?"
                    —Evelyn Mannie.

Taking Our Medicine

Willing to Trade
The doctor lightly shrugs it
     off
When I relate my misery,
And so would I without a
     sigh
If it inflicted him, not me.
                    —Paul Tulien.

Unfortunate Wording
     The sick patient,
conscience-stricken at having
summoned his doctor past
midnight, apologized profusely.
"I'm sorry about the hour,
Doc, and I know my house
is somewhat out of your way,
too."
     "Oh, that's all right,"
reassured the medico. "I have
another very sick patient who
lives near you; so I'll just kill
two birds with one stone."

Daffynitions
     Desert psychiatrist: Mirage
counselor.
                    —Daisy Brown.

     Intern: Ward healer.
                    —William LaTourette.

     Nerve specialist: Twitch
doctor.
                    —Frank Tyger.

     Physician's toupee: Medic
hair.
                    —Ralph Noel.

Taking Our Medicine

Malpractice suit: the law of the bungle.
> —John H. Dromey.

Sock It to Her!
"How can I cure my wife of snoring?" the man asked his doctor.

"By kindness, understanding, helpful advice and patience," replied the doctor.

"But I've tried all that," cried the harassed hubby.

"In that case," advised the doctor, "you might try sticking an old sock in her mouth."
> —Herm Albright.

Ill Temper
"What really drives me up the wall about doctors," a man complained, "he makes me wait six weeks to get an appointment; and then he says, 'You should have come to me sooner'."
> —Robert Orben.

Gag Rule
Here is to dentists, including
   mine,
A slight but important
   suggestion:
When your patient's mouth
Is crammed north to south,
It's best not to ask a
   question.
> —Richard Armour.

"Now your medical history—any lawsuits?"

Taking Our Medicine

Mouthing Off
Consulting with my dentist,
I told him where my doubt
    lay:
Which would be worse—the
    inlay?
Or, later on, the outlay?
          —Dick Emmons.

Emergency
A colleague called a
surgeon and asked him to
make a fourth at poker.
"Going out, honey?" his wife
asked suspiciously. The
husband answered gravely:
"Yes dear. It's an extremely
important case. Three other
doctors are there already."
          —Paul Harwitz.

Medical Note
It's hard to get a modern
doctor close enough to a bed
to tell whether he has a
good bedside manner or not.
          —H. E. Martz.

Internal Medicine?
The menu in a Midwest
medical school cafeteria offers
split-fee soup.
          —Frank Tyger.

Super-Specialists, Ltd.
Medicine has become so
    specialized these days
That doctors are taking the
    position

That if your head cold moves
    down to your chest,
You must consult another
    physician.
          —Ruth M. Walsh.

Neat Prognosis
An elderly man went to a
doctor for a check-up. The
doctor completed the
examination, then reported to
his patient, "Mr. Jones, you
will live to be eighty."
"But I am eighty!" Said Mr.
Jones.
"See?" Smiled the medic.
"What did I tell you?"
          —Lane Olinghouse.

Modern Medicine
An acupuncture surgeon
was awakened in the middle
of the night by a phone call.
Sleepily, he informed the
distressed patient: "Take two
pins and call me in the
morning."
          —Shelby Friedman.

Reverse English
"Let the buyer beware" was
    once the advice,
And the consumer came
    prepared,
But with liability suits on the
    loose,
It's the seller who's now
    running scared.
          —George O. Ludcke.

Capsule Comment
A man went to a
psychiatrist and was told the
fee would be sixty dollars an
hour. "That's okay," said the
patient, "I'll only take a
minute of your time."
          —Herm Albright.

Her Son, the Doctor
"My son is a surgeon.
He's performed over one-
thousand operations!" bragged
the proud mother. Then,
while her audience digested
this fact, she added: "And he
hasn't cut himself once!"
          —Paul Harwitz.

Medimorphosis
The family doctor
Disappeared in a wink,
And in his place
Is now MD, Inc.
          —Arnold J. Zarett.

Prescription
I told my doctor I had
the Russian flu, and he said,
"Take two vodkas and call
me in the morning."
          —Herm Albright.

Practical Medicine
A patient, who had been
given six months to live,
failed to pay his bill. So the
doctor gave him another six
months.
          —Art Jones.

Dieting

Solid Statistic
The number of Americans who are overweight has now reached nearly ninety million. That's in round figures, of course.

—Robert Fuoss.

Noonsense
People whose clothes
Fit them neatly
Are usually those
Who lunch petitely.

—Mary Reeves Mahoney.

Daffynitions
Dieter: One who wishes others wouldn't laugh at his expanse.

—Al Bernstein.

Reducing salon: thinner sanctum.

—Lane Olinghouse.

Second Helpings
More Turkey means
More stuffing, means
More gravy, yams,
And butter beans,
More Hollandaise-smothered
Broccoli,
More onions, creamed—
And, alas, more me!

—Ethel Jacobson.

"Have your daly bread every **other** day for while."

Dieting

No Interruptions, Please
You can tell me of the
  hazards
Of an excess gain of weight,
Of the lean and lovely
  females
I should try to emulate.

You may stress the fact that
  munching's
Psychologically defeating,
I'll listen to your sage advice
But, please, not while I'm
  eating.
　　　　—Dorothy Dalton.

Two-Weigh Switch
A dieter, it seems, is built
With quite a fluctuating guilt:
His conscience very often
  fails,
Except when he is on the
  scales.
　　　　—G. Sterling Leiby.

Inside Job
Strategic spots I have to
  change
To measure in the normal
  range,
But exercises on the floor
Spark my hunger, make me
  sore.
And despite the daily din,
Though I push the outside in,
I seldom put the pounds to
  rout
For I get fat from inside out!
　　　　—Dorothy Dalton.

Business Man's Dilemma
He has had to buy a bigger
  belt,
As his figure has turned less
  than svelte.
Each high caloric business
  dinner
Has left him fatter, but a
  winner;
With every contract he has
  landed,
He has expanded.
　　　　—Colleen Stanley Bare.

Image Note
A dieting woman's best
motive is sylph-preservation.
　　　　—H. E. Martz.

Weight-Watcher's Lament
When I'm trying to get
  thinner
People ask me out to dinner.
But when I need no longer
  diet,
What do I get? Peace and
  quiet.
　　　　—Robert Fuoss.

Domestic License
Dinner for one, please James,
Madam will not be eating.
She's gone on one of her
  diets
And is in the kitchen—
  cheating.
　　　—Marguerite Whitley May.

Stout Reminder
Many of us are
discovering that raiding the
larder has a tendency to lard
the raider.
　　　　—Diantha W. Adler.

Daffynitions
Obesity: fat accompli.
　　　　—Len Elliott.

Reducing diet: taming of
the chew.
Glutton: abdominal stow
man.
　　　　—Shelby Friedman.

Stiff Problem
Some dieters go starch-
craving mad.

Future Fullfiliment
I've learned that once again I
  must,
Partake of foods which taste
  like dust,
And sort of self-disintegrate
By taking off a lot of weight.
Although the future now
  looks black—
What fun 'twill be to put
  pounds back!
　　　　—Bert H. Kruse.

Victual Ritual
Most people will cheat on a
  diet,
But my position's unique;
For I follow mine religiously,

Dieting

With one day of observance
   per week.
          —Edward F. Dempsey.

Retention Requirement
I wish that I could retain,
Through a herculean feat,
As much of what I read
As I do of what I eat.
          —Ramona Demery.

Nutrition Note
Remember the old days
when a liquid protein diet
was chicken soup?
          —Gil Stern.

Pot Pourri
My penalty for pastries—
Rolls or muffins, cold or hot,
Is the burden of carrying with
   me
A bloomin' flour pot.
          —T.B. Sennett.

Dietribes
["American diets today are
high in proteins, fats and
controversy."—WSJ headline.]
I eat all sorts of food
Without any concern;
It's the controversy
That gives me heartburn.
          —Arnold J. Zarett.

Weighty Words
I've talked a lot about diets
The experts have proposed,

But the real way to lose
Is to keep the mouth closed.
          —Ramona Demery.

Nutty Knowledge
Compulsive eater: a
person who puts his mania
where his mouth is.
          —Shelby Friedman.

Imbibing

Bourbon Development
A Louisville cocktail party
was in full swing and one of
the celebrants seemed to be
getting a mite unsteady on
his feet. Seeking to avoid an
embarrassing scene, a still-
sober guest said to the host:
"Colonel, our friend seems to
have had a bit too much
julep."
"Suh," drawled the
colonel, "You may think him
drunk—but in Kentucky we
call that bein' in mint
condition."
          —Robert Fuoss.

Daffynitions
Whiskey truck: mash
transportation.
          —Raymond J. Cvikota.

Cocktail glasses: hic cups.
Club car: cabooze.
          —Honey Greer.

Hangover: the moaning
after.
          —Carroll S. Karch.

Hangover: Brewtality.
          —H. E. Martz.

Teetotaler: draught dodger.
          —Mary Lee Sauermann.

Imbibing

BURBANK

"Full-bodied, with a bold and rather presumptuous bouquet, wouldn't you say?"

No Contest
I quit because I realized
How better off I'd be.
The stuff I drank to turn me
on
I found just turned on me!
—Ralph Shaffer.

You Can't Win
The curse of not drinking,
To my way of thinking,
Is the constant explaining
Of why you're refraining.
—F. G. Kernan.

Liquor Authority
Alcohol is something an adolescent drinks to prove he is an adult, and an adult drinks to prove he is an adolescent.
—H. E. Martz.

Sign Language
Posted over the bar in a neighborhood saloon: "Abstinence Is a Good Thing, but Should Be Practiced in Moderation."
—Dan Janson.

Daffynitions
Tequila: The Gulp of Mexico.
—Raymond J. Cvikota.

Beer ad: brewprint.
—John Dratwa.

Imbibing

Cocktail party at Indian
Embassy: Gin and tunics.
— Murray Cohen.

Teetotaler: One who is
conspicuous by his abstinence.
— F. G. Kernan.

Skid row: bottleground.
— Dave Lande.

Pink elephants: beasts of
bourbon.
— Honey Greer.

Russian pub: little red
skoal house.
— Bert Murray.

Hangover: Binge twinge.
— Lane Olinghouse.

Liquidate: Invitation to a
cocktail party.
— Gertrude Pierson.

Sobriety test: Rye detector.
— Jane Hunt Clark.

Tipsy Scale
"One out of 20
Americans drinks to excess, a
study reveals."— News Note.
The million people the victims
Of alcoholic rigors?

Most observers would concede
That those are staggering
figures!
— George O. Ludcke.

Opening Round
What is it makes champagne
so great,
What lends that special
touch?
Is it the bubbles, coolness,
taste,
Or that it costs so much?

No, I believe it's none of
these,
Or each the merest token.
I'd say: relief the cork is out,
None hurt, and nothing
broken.
— Richard Armour.

Nordic Nonsense
Dry Scandinavian friends of
mine,
Formerly bibulous chaps,
Tell me that during their
skoal days
A lot of their courses were
schnapps.
— Henry Barton.

Pub Crawler's Plea
Oh, dark streaked sky
In your ominous splendor,
Guide me home tonight
Before I bend a fender!
— Mike Cusack.

Insomnia

Open-Eyed Observation
Insomnia would be no plight
If just it didn't come at night.
Insomnia we'd thank and hail
If it but came, and without fail,
When there's some boring
work to do
Just after lunch, perhaps at two.
— Richard Armour.

Fitting Reprisal
It's two in the morning,
My eyelids slump low—
But (helpless) I'm watching
The Late Late Late Show.

The punishment waiting
Tomorrow is mine;
I'll have to look bright-eyed
At quarter to nine.
— Robert Gordon.

Insomnia-yak
Why is it that the person
who couldn't sleep last night
always seems so proud of it?
— Anna Herbert.

That Critical Point
I always live
From day to day;
As for tomorrow—
Let come what may.

Think only of now,
Not tomorrow, I've learned,
But around midnight
I do get concerned.
— Arnold J. Zarett.

TM—Om on the Range

"There's a fine line between meditating and snoozing."

Stuck On Yoga
Right now I am in
A dreadful condition:
I can't get out of
My lotus position.
—Mimi Kay.

T.M. in the P.M.
I've taken up meditation!
I sized it up and surmised:
Here's one way of doing
nothing
Without being criticized.
—Gail Cooke.

Inward, Not Onward
This is our decade of
discontent
As we seek the selves we've
never known
Through Yoga, Buddhism,
TM, Zen—
We're all in this together—
alone!
—May Richstone.

Idol Chatter
Gurus and cultists the kids
idolize,
To me talk tiresome pap,
But perhaps I'm just a victim
Of the veneration gap.
—Edward F. Dempsey.

Cool It
Transcendental meditation
Is that psychological bit where
The relaxing philosophy seems
to be

TM—Om on the Range

"Don't just do something—sit
    there!"
                    —George D. Ludcke.

Free and Easy
Some find contentment in
    meditation,
Listening to their gurus
    expound,
Or from yoga or encounter
    groups,
Of which there are plenty
    around.
But I've found a road to
    tranquility,
Whose virtues I'm extolling,
It's just thinking of all the
    money
I've saved by not enrolling.
                    —Edward F. Dempsey.

They Guru on You
Some Oriental philosophies
Are frankly beyond my ken,
But it's fun to explore them
    occasionally
(At least, every Mao and Zen).
                    —George O. Ludcke.

Help!
There's transactional analysis
Or transcendental meditation,
Screaming, yoga or encounters
For depression or agitation.
The choices are wide-ranging
For one's hangups or ruts,
But deciding on the right one
Can drive a person nuts.
                    —Arnold J. Zarett.

Foods—Convenient and Inconvenient

While We May
With food so full of additives
And water downright scary,
Time may be running out,
    my friend,
So eat, drink and be wary.
                    —Ellie Womack.

Tome on the Range
["*A Boon in Cookbooks
Delights Publishers—Entire
Volumes are Devoted to
Soybeans, Beer, Curries—"—
WSJ headline.*]
Oh, give me a book
That will tell how to cook
So that Escoffier'd be in awe;
I am always in need
Of light fiction to read
While I wait for my dinner to
    thaw.
                    —E. V. Girand.

Food for Thought
The rise of fast food
    restaurants,
Through convenient in many
    respects,
Is sure to increase the
    sightings of,
Unidentified Frying Objects.
                    —Edward F. Dempsey.

Look, No Calories
The staff of life,
Once hearty fare,
Is cotton gauze now,
Mostly air.
Such plastic-foam,

Pneumatic bread
Should stay on grocers'
Shelves instead,
Unless you need
A loaf for fluffing
A pillow that
Has lost its stuffing.
                    —Ethel Jacobson.

Hope for the Polluted
One day we might discover
That additives are a plus;
Together with preservatives
They're what's sustaining us.
                    —May Richstone.

Sweet Talk
Syrup from maple sugar
With flapjacks is quite
    delicious,
But the sap must be taken
    from the tree
In a manner that's
    syruptitious.
                    —George O. Ludcke.

Unpalatable Presentation
The frozen pie
You're moved to buy
By the color photo
That dazzles your eye
On the gaudy package
For which you fall,
Believe me, won't look
Like that at all!
But still, what's important
Is, how does it taste?
You want to know?
Like library paste.
                    —Ethel Jacobson.

Foods—Convenient and Inconvenient

"Two breakthroughs—imitation eggs made of soybeans and imitation soybeans made of eggs."

Food for Thought
For most young mothers,
It's true, though tacit,
The art of cooking's
A frozen asset.
     —E. B. de Vito.

Give And Take
As a natural cereal devotee,
Something I've wondered
 about,
Is how prices keep getting
 higher
As more additives come out.
    —Edward F. Dempsey.

Contents Noted
This packaged pudding from
 the store
Makes nice dessert, they say.
 What's more,
It whips up fast—in half a
 minute!
(I wish I could pronounce
 what's in it!)
     —Ing Smith.

Spicy Story
 ["*Does Your Paprika Get Up Off the Plate and Walk Away? Spices With Insects or Mold Are Coming Under Attack*"—WSJ headline]
With fungus, larvae, dirt and
 worse,
Our condiments are rife;
In short, our spices now
 contain
A variety of life.
     —E. V. Girand.

Foods—Convenient and Inconvenient

Necessary Evil?
Putting additives in food
Is one act I don't favor,
But they're needed to
    preserve
The artificial flavor.
                —Arnold J. Zarett.

Bake Off
    Now there's a bakery that
is offering a tranquilizer. It's
called pie a la mood.
                —Shelby Friedman.

Daffynition
    Coffee house: perking lot.
                —Walter Anthony.

Horse Sense
I've read of the benefit fiber
    food brings
And firmly believe what the
    doctors are saying.
I'm eating such wheaty and
    oatmealy things
That one of these days, I
    expect, I'll be neighing.
                —Irene Warsaw.

Inside Information
The Government watches with
    care what we eat
And bans what might do us
    harm,
Such as saccharin and the
    additives
That are now being viewed
    with alarm.

Since it's our insides that
    cause such concern,
The treatment might be
    superior
If the task were done not by
    HEW
But the Department of the
    Interior.
                —Richard Armour.

Sweet Truth?
    [*"Can chocolate turn you
into a criminal? Some experts
say so."—WSJ item.*]
Chocolate make you a
    criminal?
The idea's a chiller.
So here's hoping men and
    women'll
Make theirs vanilla.
                —Leonard Dittell.

Food Pan
Eating at fast-food restaurants,
Still drives me to distraction,
But I wouldn't call it snobbery,
Just a kind of gut reaction.
                —Edward F. Dempsey.

Banner Year
Saccharin isn't good for you;
Certain dyes are suspect, too.
Disaster lurks in pesticide;
Cyclamates are vilified.
If ingested by the ton,
Anything kills anyone,
Yet each day some caveat
Is issued at the drop of a rat.
                —E. V. Girand.

Ounce of Prevention
I've studied the additives
    issue,
And though my research may
    be crude
My statistics definitely show
We may have to give up
    food.
                —Arnold J. Zarett.

Saccharine Solution?
Wouldn't it really be simpler
For our illustrious
    commonwealth
Just to isolate and label the
    things
NOT injurious to health?
                —Ruth M. Walsh.

Food Fear
If something I like
Isn't harmful, I'll bet
It's only because
They've not tested it yet.
                —Ellie Womack.

Sporting Life

"It's a fuzzy tufted bird peeper."

Fore

Voice coming out of the golf course brush: "Never mind the ball, caddie, come and find me!"

—Tom Fallon.

No Winning

When a man's golf score is below ninety, he is neglecting his business; if above it, he is neglecting his game.

Fore Thought

Golfing takes energy, also
  cash—
(Just two of the things you
  must bring it);
A golf club's a great
  institution
If you are able to swing it!

—George O. Ludcke.

Exercise in Futility

The golf course being rather
  far,
I have an excuse to take the
  car,
And since the holes are far
  apart,
I have an excuse to use a
  cart.
But one thing has me still
  defeated—
You cannot hit the ball while
  seated.

—Donna Evleth.

Sporting Life

Daffynitions
Golfing vacations: tee leaves.
—Raymond J. Cvikota.

Golf trophy: proof of the putting.
—Shelby Friedman.

Nineteenth hole: bar for the course.
—Robert Fitch.

Dedicated golfer: Divotee.
—Charles M. McGee Jr.

Fairway or Freeway?
The golf course on weekends presents
A scene that is certainly graphic:
Golfers in golf carts lined up
In bunker-to-bunker traffic.
—Richard Armour.

Iron Clad Role
You show me a man with two feet planted firmly on the ground and I'll show you a man making a crucial putt on the 18th hole.
—Herm Albright.

Tee Totaler
After a fruitless and thoroughly unproductive day on the golf course, the man snarled at his caddy: "You must be the world's worst caddy!"
"But, sir," protested the boy dryly, "wouldn't that be too much of a coincidence?"
—Will Powers.

Fore-warned
The easiest way for a duffer to get out of the rough is unobserved.
—Franklin P. Jones.

Real Calculator
A Sunday golfer was attempting to choose a caddy from a group of young local lads at the local municipal course.
"You, with the red hair, how much is five, six and three?"
"Eleven," replied the boy.
"Close enough," said the golfer. "You'll do."
—Herm Albright.

Green and Bear It
I have one fault when I play golf,
I readily admit it.
I find I'm too close to the ball—
I mean after I hit it!
—Maurice Seitter.

Schuss!
Hurtling down an icy slope,
'Round icy hummocks weaving—
Such enthusiasm can only attest
That skiing is believing.
—George O. Ludcke.

Snow Jitters
My balance is wobbly,
My heart's in my mouth;
My knees have gone knobbly
My poles have gone South.
Stark fear has obsessed me,
I think I may freeze;
Whatever possessed me
To strap on these skis?
—Betty Billipp.

Bad Timing
My annual ski vacation,
As if by law,
Always coincides with
The mid-winter thaw.
—Edward F. Dempsey.

Daffynition
Ski lift: queasy chair.
—E. R. Mead.

Finny Girl
Two women were discussing the fishing trip from which their husbands had just returned.
"Honestly," sighed one, "I don't know which is worse—for Henry to catch the fish I have to clean, or lose fish I have to hear about!"
—Lane Olinghouse.

Sporting Life

Disposition Data
What fishermen and hypochondriacs have in common: they don't really have to catch anything to be happy.

—Robert Orben.

Straight Stuff
Here's a truth men can
  perceive
As wholly everlasting:
Oh, what a tangled web they
  weave
When first they practice fly
  casting.

—Annis Poland.

Poor Sport
Two old friends went fishing. For many hours they perched lazily on a bridge, drinking one beer after another as they waited for the fish to bite.

One of them, after a long swallow of brew, said, "Whoever gets the first bite, I betcha it'll be me!" Whereupon, he fell off the rail and into the creek.

"Hey," yelled his friend, "if you're gonna dive for 'em, the bet's off!"

Tennis Tip
Though your game is hardly
  the best,
You can fray your opponent's
  nerves
By methodically bouncing the
  ball
At least 10 times before your
  serves.

—Arnold J. Zarett.

Daffynition
Tennis pro: lob technician.

—Raymond J. Cvikota.

Buyer Beware
I buy all "inner" books about
  racquet, driver and putter,
Then out on the court and
  links I find I still fret and
  mutter.
I'm at a loss to explain why
  I can't be a winner
After providing the authors
  with their inner dinner.

—J. M. de Jong.

Semantically Speaking
If you have a hobby, the
  name you are called
Is quite simple, or somewhat
  bravado—
Depending on whether you're
  low-brow or high
It's "buff" or "aficionado."

—G. O. Ludcke.

Arch Villain
He played a crooked croquet
  game.
His tactics were hardly cricket,
Each stroke had mallets
  aforethought
An his strategy was wicket.

—George O. Ludcke.

Progress Note
A nice thing about bowling
—it gets kids off the streets
and into the alleys.

—Tiny Griffith.

Status Borrowed
A tennis court is great,
So is a heated pool.
With a good-sized sauna
One can play it cool.

But I don't like to fuss,
Nor do I follow trends;
My status symbol's that
I find them at my friends.

—Arnold J. Zarett.

Touch of Humility
A boat can be a humbling
  force
As well as an escape:
The owner very quickly learns
To kneel, scrub, bow and
  scrape.

—E.B. de Vito.

Good Sport
He drives a sports car and
  he takes sporting chances.
He wears a sport coat that's
  well fitting.
He reads the sports page and
  he sports a mustache
And his favorite sport is
  sitting.

—Richard Armour.

Sporting Life

"Your first boat?"

Measure of the Ego
Well-adjusted person: one who can play golf and bridge as if they were merely games.

Puzzler
I find no place to use 'em,
Those entrancing verbs and
    nouns,
Except just where I found
    'em
In crossword ups and downs.
    —Marjorie McEwan Haller.

For External Use Only
"That champagne you sent us to celebrate our winning the pennant," the baseball club owner complained to the manager of the liquor store, "was pretty foul stuff!"

"Good heavens!" the liquor man gasped, "I thought you were just going to pour it over each other!"
    —Edward Stevenson.

White on White Sail
Romantic sailors at the helm
Are eager to take flight,
They hoist their sails,
When the wind prevails
And leave port at dawn's
    early light,

All day they ply the heavy
    seas
Frolicking on the briny,
"Oh God, your ocean is oh
    so big,

Sporting Life

And my boat is oh so tiny."

Then suddenly the wind turns
    fierce,
Perhaps it's just to remind
    them,
It's time to go home on the
    angry foam,
Wagging their sails behind
    them.
        —Peter Lind Hayes.

Brave on Blades
Some skaters do a Figure
    Eight;
I can't do even Seven—
But, knowing that I'm
    tempting fate,
I sometimes try Eleven.
        —Dick Emmons.

Daffynitions
Featured wrestling match:
maim event.
        —Edward Stevenson.

Famous daredevil's earnings:
thrill-gotten gains.
        —Shelby Friedman.

Racetrack: Horsing
development.
        —Daphne Brown.

Hockey puck: Slapped disc.
        —Raymond J. Cvikota.

Boxing arena: Champsite.
        —Daisy Brown.

Athletic field: limber yard.
        —Antoni Tabak.

Karate School: Chopping
Center.
        —Paul Harwitz.

Kentucky: foal's paradise.
        —Frank Tyger.

Bird Watcher: trill-seeker.
        —Paul Harwitz.

Hockey match: the war
between the skates.
        —Frank Tyger.

Hang-glider club: soarority.
        —John Dratwa.

Life-long polo playing:
chukkered career.
        —Bert Murray.

Board Reward
Skateboard owners—
Youthful speedists!—
Bring swift joy to
Orthopedists.

What the young may
Feel as raptures,
Medics treat as
Forearm fractures.
        —Robert Gordon.

Truth Capsule
Gambling is getting
something for nothing—no
matter how much it costs.
        —Franklin P. Jones.

Chrono-Logic
He passed the Dangerous
    Forties
Without being led astray;
The Fearsome Fifties found
    him sound;
The Sixties were his heyday.
He took the Seventies right
    in stride,
And called fears of the
    Eighties phony;
But at ninety a fall quickly
    ended it all
(He was thrown from his
    polo pony).
        —George O. Ludcke.

Sweet Truth
Knee bends, jogging, volley
    ball—
I do these till it hurts,
But I wouldn't have to skip
    that rope
If I'd only skip desserts.
        —Rosemarie Williamson.

Occupational Hazards
You're not in style until you
    feel
The painful pangs of
    "Jogger's Heel"!
Which leads to thoughts of
    "Sprinter's Toe,"

Sporting Life

And "Housemaid's Knee"
    from long ago!

"Tennis Elbow," "Swimmer's
    Ear"—
"Preachers Throat's" a mess I
    hear!
"Skier's Leg" requires a cast,
"Wrestler's Ribs" hurt while
    they last!

"Athlete's Foot" entails no
    stiches,
Does involve horrendous
    itches!
Hate to stop, but (serves me
    right)
I've "Writer's Cramp," And so
    good night!
            —Marjorie Connelly.

III THE YEAR

"We used to go to Capistrano but it got so crowded we started going to the Ozarks."

The Seasons

"Nearly spring—the best part of the year. Smack dab between the roar of the snowblowers and the snarl of the power mowers."

Late October Rhyme
Hickory, dickory, dock,
It's time to set back your
    clock;
If you should forget
You'll not be, I'll bet,
The only oddball on your
    block.
                    —G. Sterling Leiby.

Fed Up!
It's well that they made it the
    shortest month
Winter gets pretty dreary—
And those of us birds who
    can't fly south
Get a bit Febru-weary.
                    —George O. Ludcke.

August
Poor little August;
Let's pause for a minute
To honor the month
With no holidays in it.
                    —Gloria Rosenthal.

April Showers
The raining is raining all
    around
On every living thing.
It falls on trees and shrubs
    and ground—
And, soddenly, it's Spring!
                    —Suzanne Douglass.

Suspense
The saddest sound of
    summer,
As you lie in bed at night,

The Seasons

Is the hum of a mosquito
Picking out a landing site.
—Suzanne Douglass.

Daffynitions

Harvest time: Fodders day.
—Raymond J. Cvikota.

September Morn: The last
pose of summer.
—Ralph Noel.

End of Romance

Don't give me all that hocus-
pocus
About the robin and the
crocus;
At our house it is not the
bud
Which heralds Springtime. It's
the mud.
—Betty Billipp.

Leaves of Stress

["—*the net cooling effect
of a young, healthy tree is
equivalent to ten room-size air
conditioners.*"—*WSJ Briefs*]
Information such as this
Leaves me quite dismayed;
Something must have gone
amiss—
It's ninety in the shade!
—E. V. Girand.

Non-Workable Hint

Here's how you can easily
Tell the seasons apart:
Is it your snowblower
Or lawn mower that won't
start?
—Arnold J. Zarett.

Weather Warped

The cold winds of winter
Have always incensed me.
Wherever I'm faced, they
Are always against me.
—E. B. de Vito.

Snow Use

When the pavements are icy,
My energy's drained;
Knowing nothing ventured is
Nothing sprained!
—Jane Hunt Clark.

Ultimate Melter

Of all the snow removal
systems
That modern methods can
supply,
The simplest and the most
efficient
Is July!
—Stephen Schlitzer.

Blankety Blanket

"There's nothing in nature
more beautiful than one
snowflake," said the wife to
her husband on a wintry
afternoon.
"Yes," he muttered, gazing
out at the snow-covered
driveway," but unfortunately
they seldom come that way."
—Herm Albright.

Get the Drift?

The last vestige of winter's
snow
From the driveway and walk
have fled—
And no one regrets that the
days
Of shovelry are dead.
—George O. Ludcke.

Temperature Tantrums

When I'm South for the
winter
This comes as no surprise:
I arrive for record lows—
While back home they hit
new highs.
—Arnold J. Zarett.

Feather Report

On a cold, blustery winter
day
When the birds are huddled
together,
Do you think that by any
chance
They could be discussing the
weather?
—Maurice Seitter.

Fall Guy

Leaves turning scarlet
overnight;
Wild geese in v-formation;

The Seasons

Indian Summer's nostalgic
   glow—
Man, that's my kind of
   autumnation!
         —George O. Ludcke.

Outdoor News
   An ant just saw its
shadow—so there will be six
more weeks of picnic weather.
            —Gil Stern.

Holidays

"Now then, when did you first notice that
people were out to get all they can out of
you?"

Holidays

Modern Thanksgiving
Over the river and pay the
    toll
And don't spill the high-fibre
    casserole;
Gram's new condominium gets
    a rave
While the turkey cooks in her
    micro-wave.
            —Peg Kehret.

Christmas Unpresent
Those cards that you get
From senders you've missed
Are the ones you crossed
Off last year's list.
            —Robert Gordon.

Daffynition
    Scrooge: a rebel without a
Claus.
            —Paul Dunn.

Holiday Thrift Drift
Well-timed rifts
Save on gifts.
            —Dorothy Dalton.

Strange Coincidence
Did you ever stop and
    wonder
At fate's peculiar ways—
For nearly all our famous
    men
Were born on holidays.
            —Dick Stanzione.

Thanksgiving Dinner
I'm giving special thanks
    today;
My untold joys, expressed;
And I am not ashamed to
    say
That I am truly blessed:
I look around the table at
My family, all so dear,
And I am really thankful that
We're eating out this year.
            —Gloria Rosenthal.

Aftermath
Now that the holidays are
    over,
I'll have to get adjusted
To the peace, the quiet, the
    daily rest,
And the fact that I am
    busted.
            —Bob Brown.

Seasonal Work
Preparing for the holdiays,
She's staying home with her
    knitting.
Making gifts both thoughtful
    and apt,
But very rarely fitting.
            —Edward F. Dempsey.

Up a Tree
The Christmas tree we gaily
    buy
With festive joy and laughter
Enthralls us less when we
    must try
Disposing of it after.
            —Donna Evieth.

Seasonal Sign
    You know the holidays
are over when you see a
Christmas wreath adorning the
hood of a refuse pick-up
truck.
            —Salty Smith.

Returning Home—Spent

HOW TO STAY HOME ON $20 A DAY

COCHRAN!

Unparalleled Problem

Twixt latitude and longitude
I can't remember quite
Which of them goes up and
    down
And which goes left to right

However, I'm learning by
    degrees,
And I'd show gratitude
If this process takes too long,
That I be shown latitude.
                    —George O. Ludcke.

Global Problem

The high price of travel
    abroad.
No matter where you might
    stay,
Means any street you shop
    on,
Can be called Rue de la Pay.
            —Edward F. Dempsey.

Class Distinction

    ["Russia's Aeroflot now
offers first-class seats at higher
fares on internal flights."—
WSJ news item]
The virtuous Marxist theories
Have had a curious sequel:
Each proletarian is the same,
But some are more than
    equal.
                    —Robert Gordon.

Capsule Comment

    In the old days, if a
person missed the stagecoach
he was content to wait a day

Returning Home—Spent

or two for the next one.
Nowadays, we feel frustrated
if we miss one section of a
revolving door.
                —Doris Dolphin.

Air Fare
[*"Single huge kitchen at
JFK prepares meals for most
international airlines."—News
item*]
From Europe to Asia,
From France to Iran,
One magic chef's making
Your dinner by plan.
Whatever you're hoping
From foreign cuisines,
Those menus get cooked up
By a kitchen in Queens.
                —Robert Gordon.

Notes from Abroad
European hotels are
changing their room signs.
They used to say: "Have you
left anything?" Now they say:
"Have you anything left?"
                —Bob Orben.

Throes a Crowd!
Those major airport traffic
    jams
That make the traveler want
    to cry,
Are not the fault of those
    who go,
But those who come to wave
    goodbye!
                —Anton F. Gross.

Profit Tale
A motorist stopped at a
small town diner for breakfast
and was aghast when his bill
was presented. "Five dollars
for scrambled eggs! What's
the matter—are eggs hard to
come by in this town?"
    "No, sir," smiled the
waitress, "but tourists are."
                —Murray Cohen.

Flight Pattern
The time I've spent waiting at
    airports
Really is a crime.
It makes me think some
    airlines run,
On Eastern Stranded Time.
                —Edward F. Dempsey.

State Park Signs
The piles of empty
Cans of beer
Reveal there's been
Real wildlife here!
                —Bert Kruse.

'Way Back When
On many a congested Friday
    night,
Stranded at an airport, and
    stand-bying,
I miss the good old days of
    1950
When lots of people were
    afraid of flying!
                —Sam Hudson.

Plane Truth
As we circle the airfield
    around and around,
I have just one bee in my
    bonnet.
That thing they said never
    would get off the ground
Now can't seem to get back
    upon it.
                —Donna Evleth.

Subway: Rabid transit.
                —Jack Kraus.

Travel Note
Someday we'll be flying to
Mars for regular vacation trips.
Of course, our baggage will
probably wind up on Venus.
                —Herm Albright.

Travel writer: traipse
recorder.
                —Daisy Brown.

Labor's Love Not Lost
I spent my vacation at
    vigorous play;
I bowled and I swam with no
    interludes off.
I danced every night, and
    with dawn's early light,
Leaped up to tackle a session
    of golf.
I strained my muscles on
    tennis courts,
And hiked the trails when I
    didn't ride.
I'll own it was tough, but I

Returning Home—Spent

did my stuff
As the Recreation Director's
   pride.
Now that I'm here at my
   desk once more,
A sense of peace suffuses my
   breast.
And eases my mind. For
   back at the grind,
Maybe I'll get a little rest.
   —George Starbuck Galbraith.

Sign Language
Travel agency poster:
"Visit Hawaii on our lei-
away plan."

Ready and Waiting
I like vacations,
But if truth be told,
I find they just put
My problems on hold.
   —Arnold J. Zarett.

Winter Daze
There'll be no vacation,
We've no plans to roam;
In fact we can barely
Afford to stay home.
   —Gail Cooke.

Travelers Checked
Take a vacation to get
away from it all, and you run
into a lot of people who
want to get it all away from
you.
   —Lane Olinghouse.

Matter of Choice
At the typical vacation
resort a gal has two choices:
Slink or swim.
   —Frank Tyger.

Travel Talk
People go on vacation to
forget things—and as soon as
they open their luggage they
realized they've succeeded.
   —Paul Harwitz.

Over-Drive
Whenever our family takes a
   trip
We squabble over which
   sights to see.
Our vacation driving, it could
   be said,
Is done by a steering
   committee.
   —Edward F. Dempsey.

Daffynitions
Mt. Rushmore: rock of
sages.
   —Steve Hogue.

Ganges: swami river.
   —A. Laura.

Vacation slides: Trek
photography.
   —Raymond J. Cvikota.

Aquatics show: dive-in
theater.
   —Daisy Brown.

Tour De Farce
When a European trip I seek,
The timing always seems
   wrong,
For that's when my currency
   gets weak
While all the others get
   strong.
   —Leonard Dittell.

Traveler's Warning
Motels have designs
That are neatly arrangeable.
Throughout the whole country
They're all interchangeable.
   —Robert Gordon.

Advice to Tourists
In under-developed
countries, don't drink the
water. In developed countries,
don't breathe the air.

Castaways: two on the
isle.
   —Raymond J. Cvikota.

Flight of Imagination
The menu gives it fancy
   names
To set an exotic mood,
But when it comes, on plastic
   trays,
It's still just airplane food.
   —Donna Evleth.

Returning Home—Spent

Stray Thoughts
Down the runway
And into the sky
Watch our superjet
Rising on high.
Others may dream
Of foreign places,
Strange surroundings,
Fresh new faces.
But I'm wondering,
In that Boeing,
Where in the world
Is my baggage going?
— Robert Gordon.

Daffynition
Busy travel agency: where
money grows on sprees.
— Shelby Friedman.

Vacation Vendetta?
People who like to be where
it's at,
By way of some nefarious
plot,
Are invariably married to
People who like to be where
it's not!
— Ruth M. Walsh.

Fringe Benefit
My vacation costs grow higher
each year.
And if this trend doesn't
cease,
Next year I'll be demanding,
A cost of leaving increase.
— Edward F. Dempsey.

Rest Cure
By the time we find a
summer camp for the kids, a
kennel for the pets, a
housesitter for the house and
a plant-talker for the plants,
we may be too tired to take
our vacation after all.
— Arch Napier.

Daffynitions
Travel folder: trip tease.
— Mary Margaret De Angelis.

Travel promotions: treks of
the trade.
— Robert Fuoss.

Time Off!
For two weeks I've cooked
on open fires,
Roasted hog dogs stuck on
wires,
I've heated water for hours
and hours
To give the children makeshift
showers.
I've slept on the ground in
forest camps,
I've woken up with muscle
cramps,
And now I have the distinct
sensation
That what I need is a
vacation.
— Donna Evleth.

Daffynitions
Reservation: berth right.
— Len Elliott.

Camper: roaming house.
— Ralph Noel.

Outdoor dinner: Soup to
gnats.

Loch Ness monster: Lizard
of odds.
— Raymond J. Cvikota.

Ouch!
Her trip through the Latin
countries
Was a flop for the eager
spinster;
Despite her great expectations
It was only her shoes that
pinched her!
— G. O. Ludcke.

Valedictory
Arrivederce, my friend, au
revoir!
Auf wiedersehen, as they say
in the Saar.
Aloha! Farewell! Adios, kimo
sabe.
Saying "goodbye" could grow
into a hobby.
But after one last sayonara to
you,
I'll finish this verse without
further adieu!
— Bob McKenty.

Gardening

"Dissolve two aspirins in a pail of water, pour it around the roots and call me again in the morning."

Gulp
I loved my vegetable garden,
So here is my sad ballad:
I nurtured it for months
And ate it in one salad.
—Arnold J. Zarett.

The Growing Green
In spite of all the instructions
And all of the technical talk,
All that you need to grow
    fine green grass
Is to have a crack in your
    walk.
—George O. Ludcke.

Winged Victory?
When insects dwell inside
    your garden,
Your heart at once begins to
    harden;
You take on proprietary airs
But the bugs, you see,
    assume it's theirs.
—Rosemarie Williamson.

As Ye Sow
To enjoy the results of a
    garden—
Without work, your chances
    are slim,
Till you find a neighbor that
    has one—
And carefully cultivate him!
—George O. Ludcke.

Gardening

Seasonal Envy
All summer our neighbors
Give us no quarter—
Their grass is not only
Greener—but shorter.
            —May Richstone.

Candid Comment
            The proverb that tells us
we reap what we sow
apparently does not apply to
amateur gardners.
            —Lane Olinghouse.

Not Easily Offended
Plants won't thrive, if talked
        to crossly;
Basically, they're fragile
        breeds;
But I note, by contrast, you
        can mutter
Anything you please to
        weeds!
            —Rosemarie Williamson.

A Pox on the Vernal Equinox
I plant a garden every spring;
Start out with that vernal
        zing:
I buy my seeds, prepare the
        soil,
Don't mind the hours of
        arduous toil.
And then I carefully,
        prayerfully sow,
And wait and wait for things
        to grow;
But by the time seeds

germinate
I am ready to terminate,
For I am thoroughly
        disenchanted
With what comes up I never
        planted!
            —Ruth M. Walsh.

Rash Statements
            In these days of frozen
dinners, cake mixes and
instant coffee, poison ivy is
the only thing left that starts
from scratch.
            —W.J. Cronenberger.

Rock and Reel
I unravel the hose
To water sweet peas,
Untangle it further
To sprinkle the trees;
I'm a regular soak
In dry-weather time—
The hose isn't reeling
Half as much, though, as I'm.
            —Lenore Eversole Fisher.

Dumb Digit
I have a green thumb, as my
        neighbors all note.
In my garden you'd think me
        quite clever.
I have a green thumb, as I
        just now wrote—
It's green with envy, however.
            —Richard Armour.

Planters Punch Line
            Give a person enough
rope nowadays—and they'll
hang a basket.
            —Shelby Friedman.

Sign Language
            Letterhead on a tree
surgeon's mailing pieces:
"Trust Us to Increase Your
Leaf Expectancy."
            —Dutch Cohen.

Ground Rule
My early spring planting,
If things follow the norm,
Will be closely followed
By winter's last storm.
            —Edward F. Dempsey.

Weak Grounds
We suffer with bad backs,
Many experts suspect,
Because of the fact
That we walk erect.

But this is one theory
I can easily disprove;
After weeding on all fours
I can hardly move.
            —Arnold J. Zarett.

No Fertilizer!
An organic gardner
Is usually a whiz
At tilling it
Like it is.
            —R. M. Walsh.

Gardening

Ground Knowledge
Books on every facet of
gardening fill the bookstores.
They even have a book on
remedial weeding.
                    —Frank Tyger.

Garden of Vices
Whenever you see us among
   the herbs
Or tiptoing through the tulips,
We're looking for slugs and
   mealy bugs,
Not mint to put in our juleps.

For day after day we spray
   and dust
For aphids and beetles and
   snails and rust.
We take the pulse of the
   ailing iris
That's coming down with a
   floral virus.

A garden's a lovesome spot,
   God wot?
But who has the time to
   enjoy it,
With all of this toiling directed
   at foiling
The menaces set to destroy
   it!
            —Georgie Starbuck Galbraith.

Spring Cleanout
I wasn't born dirt poor,
But it comes as no surprise,
That each spring I'm left that
   way,
After shopping for garden
   supplies.
            —Edward F. Dempsey.

Daffynitions
Plastic evergreen: fake fir.
            —John Dratwa.

Horticulturist: rose scholar.

Backyard weeds: The plot
thickens.
            —Raymond J. Cvikota.

Dwarf chrysanthemum:
Minimum.
            —Shelby Friedman.

Gardening: root
awakening.
            —Herm Albright.

Parched plant: a frond in
need.
            —Arch Napier.

Gardner's Report
Though everybody knows
That plants mature from
   seedlings,
Weeds appear full-grown—
There's no such thing as
   "weedlings."
            —Rosemarie Williamson.

Grass Opinion
Two hours to sow it,
Two months to grow it,
Two days to hoe it.
Too weak to mow it.
            —Ellie Womack.

Let Us Spray
[*"—Risks posed by a
group of fungus-control
pesticides are being
investigated—"—WSJ item.*]
There is no need for running
   further tests;
There's not a product sold I
   haven't tried
And found quite safe to use
   on garden pests—
Not a single one of them has
   died.
            —E.V. Girand.

Sharing of the Green
Talk to your plants, the
   experts say,
Whether they're old or young.
It's no longer enough to have
   a green thumb;
You must also have a green
   tongue.
            —Jean Condor Soule.

Growing Pains
My gardening always ends in
   despair,
Since I'm stuck for the
   duration;
With a backyard plot that's
   arid,
And a fertile imagination.
            —Edward F. Dempsey.

Gardening

Green Elastic
New homeowners will find
This fact well worth knowing:
Their little lawns will seem
To stretch while they're
  mowing.
    —Arnold J. Zarett.

Mistake
"What do you think
your're doing?" the
homeowner shouted at the
young man from the nursery.
"I'm grafting a new outer
cover on this maple, sir," the
nurseryman replied. "Hang it
all!" cried the homeowner.
"You're barking up the wrong
tree!"
    —Edward Stevenson.

Comic Consultant
He posed as a tree authority,
But I felt he missed the mark
When he said you could
  always identify
A dogwood by its bark.
    —G. O. Ludcke.

Beasties

Snooty Pooch
Our Afghan hound
Just lounges around.
So nobly bred
It's gone to his head.
His languid boast:
He deigns to host
Only fleas
With pedigrees.
    —Ethel Jacobson.

Paw-etic Justice
Since every dog must have
  his day,
I think it right
That nature, in her balanced
  way,
Gave cats the night.
    —Herbert Warfel.

Animal Cracker
Now there's a proposed
health program for dogs. It's
called "Medicur."
    —Shelby Friedman.

The birds I like to watch the
  best
Are those that can be trusted
To stay in place while I get
My binoculars adjusted.
    —J. R. Quinn.

Daffynitions
Angry dolphins: cross
porpoises.
    —Leonard Dittell.

Deer crossing: the buck
stops here.
    —John S. Bowdidge.

Wild game: stalk market.
    —Raymond J. Cvikota.

Vicious dog: a rebel
bowser.
    —James E. Knowles.

Crodocile tears: a crying
sham.
    —Lane Olinghouse.

Puppy: Bone Vivant.
    —Raymond J. Cvikota.

Hibernation: bear necessity.
    —E. R. Mead.

Beehive: sting ensemble.
    —Paul Harwitz.

Zoo's Who
You ought to see the human
  zoo
Within us caged and hid.
The Ego's perched upon a
  perch,
Beneath it is the Id.

The Soul is basking sleepily,
The Psyche makes a fuss.
Come, see the zoo, but when
  you do—
Don't feed the Animus!
    —Richard Armour.

Beasties

For the Birds

We have a bird bath in our
    yard,
And birds enjoy it greatly.
We thought it was a good
    idea
But we have wondered lately.
The birds have disappointed
    us,
So far have dashed our
    hope.
We cannot get them, yet, to
    use
The wash rag and the soap.
> —Richard Armour.

Summer Snack

If they want supper,
Many birds sing for it.
Unfortunately
Mosquitoes sting for it.
> —Gail Cooke.

Snail's Trace

The snail's not known for
    grace or face
But for the slowness of its
    pace.
And something else: So you
    can find it
It leaves its crawling card
    behind it.
> —Richard Armour.

Box Lunch

    If ants are all that
industrious, how come they
have time for so many
picnics?
> —Robert Fuoss.

Beasties

On the Double
I suppose the baby llama
Has a ppapa and a mmama.
—Richard Armour.

Temperance Zone
[*"Fermented berries lead
to blotto birds."—WSJ
headline.*]
All summer long the birds
    were high,
But not, alas, up in the sky.
They switched to sozzled
    levitation
From berries rich in
    fermentation.

They made saloons of bush
and vine
Their songs became "Tweet
    Adeline."
But I'm not one who
    tolerates
These avian inebriates.

My yard for next year I'll
prepare—
They'll find just coffee berries
    there.
No drop of alcohol will spike
    them—
And listen birds! You'd better
    like them!
—Judy Michaels.

Word to the Beautiful People
If you would make the
    leopards purr,
Wear spotted coats of cloth,
    not fur!
This way you can be
    leopardized—
And not one leopard is
    jeopardized.
—Ralph Noel.

Extinct Possibility?
The dodo's extinction
Is easily solved.
He obviously chose
Not to get evolved.
—Robert Brault.

Survivor
[*"Ranchers, Conservationists
Feud Over Efforts to Reduce
Coyote Population."—News
Item*]
He survives against the
    unbeatable foe,
His howl is eerie and throaty;
He tilts against trappers
    instead of windmills—
He's the wide prairie's Don
    Coyote.
—George O. Ludcke.

Vintage Whine
Our dog is really a mixed
    breed,
We can't determine his
    handle.
He's partly hound, some
    terrier
And sort of a cocker scandal!
—Gail Cooke.

Hound Sound
My neighbor says this of his
    dog:
"His bark's worse than his
    bite."
I don't quite see how that
    could be—
He practices all night!
—Dick Emmons.

Pet Petulance
I'm always smitten
By a straight-tailed kitten,
And a Scottish terrier
Couldn't be merrier.
Even furry rabbits
Have engaging habits,
And I think of spring
When canaries sing.

But one pet I cannot
With joy espouse
Is the expectant hamster
We lost in the house.
—Jame Oppenheimer.

Independent Claws
A cat likes sofas, tables,
    chairs
For honing claws and making
    tears;
The scratching post you
    furnish her
She treats like priceless
    furniture.
—G. Sterling Leiby.

"You'll simply have to stop daylighting on
that other job, Abbott!"

Careers

"Any openings for an urban guerrilla?"

Status Report
There's always a price to pay for fame. Today it's the salaries of your press agent and P.R. man.
—Edward F. Dempsey.

Choice Lot
A teacher was asked why she preferred teaching in an elementary school. "Because that way I always know I'll have a parking space," she replied.
—Paul Harwitz.

To Whom It May Concern
["Ladder of success no longer means starting on the bottom rung and staying with it."—News note.]
Young people change companies often today;
Job-hopping expresses their preferences.
(They're afraid if they stay at one place too long
They'll end up with very few references.)
—George O. Ludcke.

Bell Ringer
There's a famous carillon maker who has become a legend in his chime.
—Shelby Friedman.

Careers

On Shaky Ground
Not everyone who enjoys
    finding fault
Is a soul with a negative
    twist.
A fault-finder could turn out
    to be, keep in mind,
A kindly seismologist.
                —Bert Murray.

Tot Shot
    Asked to define
"agriculture," the farmer's
small son replied, "agriculture
is something like farming —
only farming is doing it."
                —Lane Olinghouse.

Illuminating Thought
    We're convinced that
candle makers have the best
job. They only work on wick
ends.
                —George E. Bergman.

To Coin A Phrase
    A counterfeiter is a man
who gets into trouble by
following a good example.

Switch Hit
As a market consultant I'd
    have it made;
(It's a plan that I often
    rehearse)
If my clients were wise they
    would take my advice
(And then do just the
    reverse!)
                —George O. Ludcke.

Cook's Tour
    Italian chefs never retire.
They're just put out to pasta.
                —Shelby Friedman.

Everything in Its Place
You can tell that he's an
    executive
By his wisdom, poise and
    force.
(He also talks golf at the
    office
And business out on the
    course.)
                —George O. Ludcke.

Bottom's Up
He tried hard in his field,
With nothing much resultant,
So he chucked the whole
    thing
And became a consultant.
                —Arnold J. Zarett.

Silly Summary
    A busy archaeologist is
one who must eat his lunch
on the ruin.
                —Ralph Noel.

A Father's Lament
    If a boy wants to be a
carpenter, fine. But does he
have to go through Law
School before reaching that
decision?
                —Robert Fuoss.

Progress Note
    Just think how far we've
come in the twentieth century:
The man who used to be a
cog in the wheel is now a
digit in the computer.
                —Robert Fuoss.

Broken Record
    A disk jockey has the
only job where a man
becomes more popular by
playing favorites.
                —George O. Ludcke.

Daffynitions
    Retired bricklayer: one
who throws in the trowel.
                —Shelby Friedman.

    Minister: one who
performs faith lifts.
                —Shelby Friedman.

    Uninspired painter:
blandscape artist.
                —Vera Colyer.

    Beekeeper: unstung hero.
                —Paul Gelin.

    Hobo: compulsive rambler.
                —Shelby Friedman.

    Dress designer's talents:
the gift of garb.
                —Marvin Alisky.

Careers

Ghost-writer: spooksman.
—Paul Harwitz.

Plumber: Drain surgeon.
—James Earle Butler.

Dog breeder: Man of litters.
—Arthur P.Grossman.

Saloonkeeper: Boretender.
—Daisy Brown.

Poet Laureate: A bard in a gilded cage.
—Raymond J. Cvikota.

Prosperous trapper: Snare-do-well.
—Shelby Friedman.

Abdication: coming in out of the reign.
—Robert Fitch.

Masseur: cramp counselor.
—D.B. Brown.

Boat designer: land-escape architect.
—O.K. Barnes.

Highway planners: roads' scholars.
—Daisy Brown.

Gossip columnists; the spies of life.
—Doris Dolphin.

Shipbuilder: A man with a license to keel.
—Shelby Friedman.

Psychiatrist: cope pilot.
—Len Elliott.

Ornithologist: talon scout.
—Robert Fuoss.

Ticket cop: Windshield viper.
—Dominic Procopio.

Palm reader: handscape artist.
—Daisy Brown.

Chanteuse: wailflower.
—Daisy Brown.

Auctioneer: a man who takes you for bidder or worse.
—Frank Tyger.

Taxi driver: meterologist.
—Arnold Glasow.

Prizefight Promoter: Sock Broker.
—Maurice Seitter.

Golf course manager: keeper of lawn order.
—Erica H. Stux.

Tailor's apprentice: alter boy.
—Walter Anthony.

Bouncer: folk slinger.
—Lane Olinghouse.

Garment tycoon: thread bear.
—Daisy Brown.

Unemployed comic: bedevilled ham.
—Raymond J. Cvikota.

Clowns: that old gang of mime.
—Raymond J. Cvikota.

Muckraking journalist: friction editor.
—Herm Albright.

Sky divers: sharp chuters.
—Frank Tyger.

Plumber apprenticeship: Basic draining.
—Frank Tyger.

City planners: Blocksmiths.
—John H. Dromey.

Careers

Editor: Someone who strikes out what doesn't strike him.
—Myron A. Coler.

Archaeologist: Man on the ruin.
—Ralph Noel.

Hostile newscaster: rancor man. —D.B. Brown.

Economist: a person who talks about something he doesn't understand and makes you feel you are ignorant.
—Herbert V. Prochnow.

Secretary of Agriculture: wheat watcher.
—Edward Stevenson.

All In A Day's Work

"Skimps a bit on entertaining customers, doesn't he?"

All In A Day's Work

Voice of the People
Market research is what you call it when you already know the answer you want, but still have to hunt up the question that will produce it.
—Robert Fuoss.

Candid Comment
I'm not really lazy. It's just that most jobs are 9 to 5 and I don't like those odds.
—Bob Orben.

Life Style
The suburbs are full of white-collar employees who work a week to earn enough to hire a repairman for a day.
—Arnold Glasow.

Harvest
The early bird gets the worm. It's said.
But many a steno or clerk Discovers that in offices, The early bird gets the work.
—E.B. de Vito.

Rise and Whine
Most of us find it difficult to get up in the morning— except on those days we don't have to.
—Lane Olinghouse.

Overskill
He has such great self-confidence
It's really past endurance;
For even when he's wrong, it is
With total self-assurance.
—A.S. Flaumenhaft.

Take Your Choice
All of us take our position
In life's passing parade each day;
There are only three options open;
Follow, lead, or get out of the way.
—George O. Ludcke.

Loyalist
There's a bureaucratic stereo fan who won't play anything but red tapes.
—Edward Stevenson.

Resume
One of the curiosities of modern personnel practice is that starting salaries vary inversely with the length of the application you fill out to get them.
—Robert Fuoss.

Working Girl's Lunch Hour
She shops in it,
She sleeps in it;
She walks, or talks
Or meets in it.
Her lunch hour is so precious that
She hardly ever eats in it.
—E.B. de Vito.

Work Quirk
When given a job to be done,
It's best not to neglect it.
I've learned that doing it fast
Leaves more time to correct it.
—R. Kuchenbecker.

Not Accident Prone
Hard work has never killed,
So goes the ancient dictum,
But why should I take the risk
Of becoming the first victim?
—William Lodge.

Forced Tyranny
If there were more self-starters, the boss wouldn't have to be such a crank.

Dictation
Two junior executives were discussing secretaries. "My wife objects to my having a good-looking secretary," the first executive complained.
"I can have a good-looking secretary if I wish," replied the second chap. "My wife only insists that he be efficient."
—Lane Olinghouse.

All In A Day's Work

As Old as He Feels
A man has seven ages,
Shakespeare wrote.
Quite true, no doubt! But
only two I note:
On gay weekends with fun
and games aplenty,
It seems my age is rather
close to twenty.
But Monday morning, waiting
at the station,
I know what's meant by
"superannuation."

Daffynitions
Company picnic: a snack
in the grass.
—Raymond J. Cvikota.

Sloppy bricklaying: trowel
and error.
—Shelby Friedman.

Over Developed
A photo-copy machine saves
time
With each copy it imparts,
Giving workers clean, clear
copies
Of recipes and diet charts.
—R.E. Marino.

No Frills
Small businessmen are
easy to spot. They're the
ones who will sell you their
products without having done
a market survey to find out
why you want them.

Double Standard
When a businessman tires of
his job
And takes a year off, it's
quite radical;
But when a professor does
likewise
It's simply his well-earned
sabbatical.
—George O. Ludcke.

Minutes Report
A committee is a group
of people who are dedicated
to a single cause: getting off
the committee.
—Mary E. Thomas.

Cut the Encouragement
The eager new clerk was
taken aside and chided by
the manager of his
department. "Hang it all,
Lawrence," the manager said,
"stop telling the customers
they're always right. They're
insufferable enough as it is!"
—Edward Stevenson.

The Lunch Crunch
This is the only country
in the world where
businessmen get together over
20-dollar steaks to discuss
hard times.
—Honey Greer.

Final Approval
A promising young
executive quit his job and,
before leaving, stopped in to
say goodbye to the boss.
"I'm sorry to see you go,"
the boss lamented. "Actually
you've been like a son to me
— sassy, impatient,
demanding."

Eager Beaver
A young man applying for
a job filled out a
questionnaire and tried to
answer every section. The
final question was: "Length of
residence at present address."
Conscientiously, he wrote
down: "Approximately forty
feet, not counting the garage."

Time Study
Patience is a much-
admired virtue, but the only
truly patient men seem to be
those who are being paid by
the hour.

Campus Comment
Show me a college dean
whose professors are out on
strike and I'll show you
someone who's no longer in
possession of his faculties.
—Bert Murray.

Supply and Demand
Two small boys were
discussing fanciful future

All In A Day's Work

careers. One said, "I'm going to be a mind reader when I grow up."

"I'd rather read palms for a living," announced the other. "Nearly everyone has palms."

—Lane Olinghouse.

Busy Afternoon

Bending over my desk, I shuffle
The stack of reports once more,
And wish to heaven someone would muffle
The adding machine next door.

I wish I'd finished at least a third of
The work on this towering stack.
I wish an uncle I'd never heard of
Would leave me a pile of jack.

I wish I were in the mountains fishing,
Or donning my skiing gear
At St. Moritz. And while I am wishing,
I wish that I had a beer.

Lifting a languid hand that smothers
A yawn I'm obliged to block,
I wish one wish above all others:
I wish it were five o'clock!

—Georgie Starbuck Galbraith.

Work Schedule

There's a time for typing
And a time to scribble;
There's a time for griping
And a time to nibble.
There's a time to stand
And a time for sitting;
But the time that's grand
Is the time for quitting!

—G. Sterling Leiby.

Tranquilizer

No pill can relax
The office bunch
Like the boss not returning
After lunch.

—E.B. de Vito.

Proper Monster

One farmer was telling another about a marvelous scarecrow he had devised. It was made of tin and not only waved its arms but also emitted a blood-curdling yell every few minutes.

"Yeah, but does it really scare the crows?" his neighbor demanded.

"I'll have you know," the proud farmer replied, "that it scares them so bad they bring back the corn they stole last year!"

—Herm Albright.

Aide Memoire

In choosing an assistant, these
Are needs I underline:

He must know how to do his job
But not try to get mine.

—Lester A. Sobel.

Friday's Flaw

Of working days, each Friday is
The best of all the five;
The thing that aches is that it takes
All week long to arrive.

—Dick Emmons.

Organizer

The nice thing about making lists
Of jobs that I have perking
Is, by the time the list is done
It's too late to start working!

—C.M. Bryant.

Weekly Meeting

Monday morning, you're too soon!
I'm not ready for you yet.
I've a weekend to forget;
Can't you wait at least till noon?
Better still, get lost, old blues day,
Let me start my week with Tuesday!

—G. Sterling Leiby.

Qualifications

After nervously clearing his throat and assuming a

All In A Day's Work

"Sit anywhere. We're equal opportunity
employers."

firm stance, the hired hand said to his boss, "I've been with you twenty-five years and I've never asked for a raise before."

The farmer replied, "Wal, Clem, that's why you've been with me for twenty-five years."

Cold Comfort

Labor's and management
  dislikes
Dismay me more and more;
The only place I'm free from
  strikes
Is in my bowling score.
           —Avery Giles.

Traitor

A young chap applying for work on a dairy farm was asked by the farmer, "do you have any bad habits? Do you smoke, drink or stay out late?"

"Oh, no, sir, none of those!" replied the prospective employee. "But I do one thing I think you ought to know about. I eat margarine."

Labor Pain

A day of worry is more exhausting than a week of work.
           —Jon Lubbock.

All In A Day's Work

Mixed Meanings
Drudgery: Working like a dog for money.

Hobby: Doing it for nothing.

—Frank Rose.

Ill-Advised
Of the difficult tasks in a
    fellow's life,
The toughest of all by far
Is trying to make it sound
    like you're sick
When you phone the office
    you are.

—Stephen Schlitzer.

Interrogation Pitch
When calling Mr. Jones,
I find it most appalling
To have his secretary ask:
"May I ask who is calling?"

One of these days,
When I find this all too
    taxing
I'll come right back at her
    and say:
"May I ask who is asking?"

—Raymond A. Klebba.

Sneaky Pique
Rarely are we bilked by
    people
We consider smarter or
    keener—
It's the fellow we regard as
    stupid
Who takes us to the cleaner!

—Ruth M. Walsh.

Shop Talk
Overheard at a convention attended by antique dealers: "So what else is old?"

—Silas Shay.

Daffynitions
Tough job foreman: languish barrier.

—Daisy Brown.

Personnel Department: the hire-archy.

—Raymond J. Cvikota.

Farmers' disagreements: organic feuds.

—Tony Joy.

Motivation
The young man burst into the boss's office. "I'll have to have a raise, sir. There are three companies after me."

Impressed, the boss demanded of the young executive, "What three, may I ask?"

"Light, telephone and water!"

—Herm Albright.

Sudsy Comment
After performing in another episode of a soap opera, the actor remarked to his wife: "Another day, another dolor."

—Ralph Noel.

Basic Truth
It takes longer for the meteorologist to forecast the weather these days. He has to consult more and more instruments before he takes a guess.

—Franklin P. Jones.

Help Wanted
The president of the firm called in the personnel manager and requested that he find him a new secretary.

"I want one who's efficient, a hard worker, a good typist, excellent at shorthand—and above all, I want one who is over fifty years of age," he told the personnel manager.

"Yes, sir," replied the manager, "and does your wife insist that she wear glasses, too?"

—F.G. Kernan.

Alarm Setting
Everything has to be done
    right now—
Double-time, make it quick!
We're on such a fast-moving
    schedule
Even clocks have a nervous
    tic!

—George O. Ludcke.

Nervous in Service
"Can you tell me why you feel insecure in your

All In A Day's Work

job?" the personnel counselor asked the troubled young executive.

"Well, it's hard to explain," the young man replied. "I like my work, I like the company. I just wish they'd stop issuing my desk calendar a week at a time."

—Robert Fuoss.

Truth Capsule

It isn't the hours you put in. It's what you put in the hours.

—Mae Maloo.

But We Will Now!

Do you want to start wrong
  with the new boss—
And really make him sore?
When he asks you to do
  something his way, say
"We never did it that way
  before!"

—G. O. Ludcke.

Sign Language

Posted in the window of a Laundry: "Your Clothes Are Not Torn By Machines. We Do It All By Hand."

—Paul Harwitz.

The Minor Details

When the big shots have
  signed the contract
It seems something of a pity
That they leave the hard

work to the small fry,
But refer to it as nitty gritty.

—G. O. Ludcke.

Wash Words

At the sink, in the
  washrooms,
It's never failed me yet.
I find there are no more
  towels
After my hands are wet.

—Donna Evleth.

Stand Up and Be Counted!

Some few may strike it rich,
  but we'd
Accept it on authority
That if at first you don't
  succeed,
You're with the vast majority!

—Harold Willard Gleason.

Pulp and Circumstance

[*"Ninety percent of all filed material over a year old is never referred to again."—News note.*]
If the nation's worthless paper
  is burned,
There'll be some huge funeral
  piles;
Old folders never die, they
  just
March off in single files.

—George O. Ludcke.

Intelligence Item

Occupational hazard defined: the danger of being

referred to a job when you go for your unemployment insurance check.

—William Lodge.

Special Handling

An antique dealer, moving his shop, told the moving man to be particularly careful with a vase because it was two-thousand years old. "Don't worry," the mover replied. "I'll be as careful of it as if it were new!"

—Herm Albright.

Clarity Capsule

A conference is a meeting where people talk about what they should be doing.

—Mae Maloo.

Truth in Labeling

"Men Working, Slow"
I read as I go past;
And, as one can see,
They do not work fast.

—Mimi Kay.

Success Story

The newly-promoted
  executive's smile
Became just a little faint
When he noticed his name
  on the office door
Was in water-soluble paint.

—G.O. Ludcke.

All In A Day's Work

Daffynition

Bureaucracy: officious circle.

—Robert Fitch.

Before and After

Doctors recommend that men do at least a little work even after retirement. Employers hope they'll to a little before.

—Robert Fuoss.

Repeat Performance

"When you go in for the interview," advised the employment agent, "don't tense up. Just be yourself. Be natural."

"Be natural!" wailed the applicant. "That's how I got fired from my last job."

—Robert Fuoss.

Hard Sell

With expense accounts under
    fire,
Salesmen may soon face the
    fate
Of having to make their pitch
Without being over a plate

—Edward F. Dempsey.

On the Job

He cannot vote to raise his
    pay,
If he should strike, no one
    would care.
And yet there's this that's
good: he can't
Be fired—no one would dare.
A mixture of both irked,
    enjoyed,
Thus is it to be self-employed.

—Richard Armour.

TGIF

I checked my clips and
    rubberbands;
Put some lotion on my
    hands;
Sharpened pencils I don't use;
Paused to hear the latest
    news;
Filled the stapler; opened
    mail;
Filed two letters—and one
    nail;
Now I'm ready, I've a hunch,
To settle down and go to—
    lunch!

—Gloria Rosenthal.

Mortal Words

[*"Coming up—electronic typewriters with memories."—WSJ item*]
A typewriter with memory—
How great: But I'm not
    smitten.
I'll keep my own. It happily
Forgets the tripe I've written.

—G. Sterling Leiby.

Candid Comments

A committee is a group which thinks up work for those who are not members of the committee.

—Marvin Alisky.

An opportunist is a man who makes hay with the grass that grows under his competitors' feet.

—Theodore Rubin.

Employment Agony

Some agonize so at the
    thought of work
They spend much of their
    time in flight of it.
No one ever died from work,
    they say,
But many have died from
    fright of it.

—G.O. Ludcke.

Cringe Benefit

Vacations are a corporation's way of reminding you that you're replaceable.

—Robert Fuoss.

Daffynitions

Real estate special: flaunted house.

—Shelby Friedman.

Personnel shuffle; mixed demotions.

—Daisy Brown.

All In A Day's Work

Telephone conglomerate: ding dynasty.
—Joyce Dillingham.

High-pressure salesmanship: pitchcraft.
—Honey Greer.

Q. and A.
A recent college graduate applied for a job with a data processing firm. He was given an aptitude test on which the first question was, "What does Cybernetics mean to you?"

"It means," he wrote, "that I'd better look some place else for a job."
—Robert Fuoss.

Comparison Resting
When you observe how little some people work you wonder how they will know when they have retired.
—Lane Olinghouse.

Incentive System
Deadlines can be a drag, and often
Result in work that's inferior;
But if there was no deadline to meet
I'd never get off my posterior.

Frightening Enlightening
[*Annual report writers often conceal rather than reveal essential facts, says corporation critic.*"—*News Item*]
Some who prepare financial reports,
According to those who accuse 'em,
Operate on the philosophy,
"If you can't convince 'em, confuse 'em."

All the Difference
When I haven't done all my homework
And I'm suffering mental congestion,
I stall for time with the well known line:
"Now that's a very good question!"
But when I've got all the answers
And feel equal to the task,
I can hardly wait to expostulate,
"I thought you'd never ask!"
—George O. Ludcke.

Corporate Matrimony
The merger of companies
Is just like wedlock;
They may not trade vows,
But they do exchange stock.
Some employees, like children,
Suddenly feel insecure;
The marriage, they opine,
Will not prove a cure.
But more often than not,
With objections dulled,
The participants woo—
Then have it annulled.
—Arnold J. Zarett.

Perk Up
A busy executive rang for his secretary and demanded to know where his pencil was. "Behind your ear, sir," she said. "Come on, now," the executive said impatiently. "You know I'm busy. Which ear?"
—Lucille S. Harper.

Reverse English
When freight is moved in a box car
It's a shipment, and wouldn't you know
When it's transported in a ship
It's referred to as cargo.
—George O. Ludcke.

Task Force
If anything is worth doing, it is worth telling someone how to do it well.
—Franklin P. Jones.

No Accident
In the age-old struggle to earn a buck,
It's amazing how hard work brings such good luck!
—G.O. Ludcke.

Coffee and Other Breaks

"Hoskins, we'd all like to drop bags of water on people, but there's work to be done."

Tense Situation
I can't afford this big expense
A coffee break? Why, that's a
    joke!
Why don't we simply change
    the tense
From "coffee break" to
    "coffee broke?"
          —Eleanore Padnos.

Excavation Sights
I always stop to marvel
At the great skill it takes—
Such huge holes dug by men
Forever on coffee breaks.
          —Arnold J. Zarett.

Long Ago and Far Away
Don't knock the Puritan ethic
Hard work for hard work's
    sake;
With it they built a new
    nation
Without taking a coffee break!
          —G.O. Ludcke.

Fringe Benefits
The president of a
company was about to make
an address. It had been
rumored that a new stock
purchase plan was in the
offing, so his remarks were
awaited with keen anticipation.
"I am pleased to inform
you all," he said, "that your
company has come up with a
new stock purchase plan.

Coffee and Other Breaks

After careful deliberation we have decided that from now on all employees will call their brokers on their own time."
—Irving Silverstein.

Break Up
One of the worst things about retirement is that you have to drink coffee on your own time.
—Paul Harwitz.

Daffynition
Water cooler: thirst aid kit.
—Steven Stegeman.

Tiff Time?
Coffee breaks
Are further extended
By the time it takes
For the break to be mended.
—Richard Armour.

Bad Break
One of two things I've
    noticed
Puts an end to a coffee
    break;
The supply of coffee runs out
Or the boss decides to
    partake.
—Richard Armour.

Speech, Speech!

"Of course I mince words, young man—it makes them easier to eat if I have to eat them later."

Speech, Speech!

Dais Light
Careful research proves that it takes a master of ceremonies fifteen minutes to introduce the man who needs no introduction.
—Robert Fuoss.

Conversation Piece
Many who have the gift of gab do not know how to wrap it up.
—Arnold Glasow.

Forced Attention
At a businessman's luncheon, a dull speaker said to the man next to him, "I can't tell you how much I appreciate your sticking around to hear the end of my speech. Most of the others seem to have left."

"Don't mention it," came the reply. "I'm the next speaker."
—Pru Pratt.

Meringue Harangue
The man who starts his
   speech while I
Am not yet finished with my
   pie
Should be aware (let me alert
   him)
That I will probably dessert
   him.
—Dick Emmons.

Daffynition
Public Auditorium: room for rant.
—Robert Fuoss.

Audience Reaction
A speaker was addressing a group of businessmen when the public address system stopped working. Raising his voice, the speaker asked a man in the back row if he could hear.

"No," the man said.

"I can hear!" shouted another man, standing up in the front row. "I'll trade places with you!"
—Herm Albright.

Speech Problem
If often happens that the man who needs no introduction is in desperate need of a conclusion.
—Robert Fuoss.

Err-ing Man
As modern speakers hem and
   haw,
You don't need much
   acumen
To verify that age-old saw—
To er-r-r is all too human.
—Charlotte Greenspan.

No Sense of Balance
Some folks can't omit details,
And their stories make one
yawn;
These people never seem
   aware
Their accounts are overdrawn.
—Rosemarie Williamson.

The Unspeakable Truth
The human brain is quite
   complex;
Its performance is truly
   unique.
It works at birth and never
   stops
Until you rise in public to
   speak.
—Ron Kuchenbecker.

The Impossible Dream
In our sleep we encountered a toastmaster at a political banquet who called on one of the guests to "say a word." The guest rose, said "Hi," and sat down.
—Edward Stevenson.

Truth Capsule
When someone says he's going to make a long story short, you can be sure the short version is going to be pretty long, too.
—Franklin P. Jones.

Wind Song
The trouble with some people who don't have much to say is that you have to listen so long to find that out.

Traffic Jams

"I ain't asking for immunity, but I do feel that all this traffic delay should be deducted from my sentence!"

Horn Aplenty
I guess it happens every
    where,
From Anaheim to Yonkers;
You yield to fellow motorists —
Behind, you get the honkers.
            —Rosemarie Williamson.

Daffynitions
Rush-hour: when motorists drive at a snarl's-pace.
            —Paul Harwitz.

Traffic Commissioner: Lane Brain.
    Commuting: Going Pains.
            —Ralph Noel.

A boring train ride: vapid transit.
            —Jane Otten.

Ten-lane highway: Colossus of roads.
            —Fred Swift.

Insufficient freeway lanes: the asphalt bungle.
            —Shelby Friedman.

Good Answer
When a highway construction worker was asked why all the roads leading into the town were being black-topped, he said to the

Traffic Jams

inquisitive motorist, "I guess you could call it hardening of the arteries."

—Murray Cohen.

Muddle of the Road

Many freeways have three lanes: A left lane, a right lane, and the one you're trapped in when you see your exit.

—Arch Napier.

Ideal Interim

People who drive trailers are lucky because they have a place to live while looking for a place to park.

—Henry Boye.

The Final Ticket

There are tickets to plays
And tickets to fights;
There are tickets to movies
And other delights—
Then there are those
    unwelcome vipers
We find beneath our
    windshield wipers!

—G. Sterling Leiby.

Marked for Improvement

The best way to inspire courteous treatment by other motorists is to drive a police car.

—Hal Chadwick.

Obstacle Course

Getting around a big city like New York wouldn't be so bad, except that the shortest distance between two points is usually under construction.

—Daisy Brown.

Courtest Course

No one was injured in the two-car collision, but the young driver was obviously distressed; "Oh, I'm sorry, it was all my fault!"

"Not at all," replied the victim soothingly. "It was my fault. I saw how you were driving—and if I'd had any sense, I'd have driven over the embankment to avoid you."

—Daisy Brown.

Accident Prone

The driver of a huge truck made a sudden stop and the car behind him crashed into him. Uninjured but irate, the motorist shook his fist at the truckdriver and shouted, "Why in blazes didn't you stick out your hand?"

"If you couldn't see my truck," came the reply, "how could you be expected to see my hand?"

—Murray Betts.

Bumper to Bumper

Your chances of getting through a late afternoon traffic snarl is like playing Rushing Roulette.

—Paul McCall.

Taxi Crab

I do not like the taxi's ways;
Its scornful manners I
    dispraise:
The way it rudely
    doubleparks,
And stops between the
    crosswalk marks,
And madly weaves from lane
    to lane,
And plain ignores you in the
    rain,
And rashly shoots red lights,
    and such
Shenanigans. I don't like
    much
These tricks it pulls to save a
    minute.
(Unless I'm in it.)

—G. Sterling Leiby.

Left Out

However popular he is,
However many friends are
    his,
No man can fail to feel
    bereft
In traffic, waiting to turn left.

—Donna Evleth.

Traffic Jams

Parade of Progress
Just think how highways have improved in fifty years! From country roads where two cars could not pass without colliding we've developed expressways where six cars can collide comfortably.
> —Robert Fuoss.

Collision Course?
If everything seems to be
    coming your way,
It should be pretty plain
That in this hectic day
You must be in the wrong
    lane!
> —Ruth M. Walsh.

Double Jeopardy
Motorists in northern climes
Consider it a bummer
When roads that were
    blocked by winter snows
Are closed for repairs in
    summer.
> —George O. Ludcke.

Commuters' Complaint
As transportation costs constantly increase, the only thing we have to fear is fare itself.
> —H. E. Martz.

The Computer—and other Infernal Machines

"There's nothing wrong with it.
It just doesn't like you."

The Computer—and other Infernal Machines

Demise of Surprise
Computers speed up election
   returns
When they say who'll win,
   there's no doubt of it;
They predict with precision
   the voter's decision
(And also take all the fun
   out of it!)
       —George O. Ludcke.

Carry One
Though our world is fast
   filling with speedy
   computers,
There's still one old habit that
   lingers:
When there's a real need for
   an answer right now
Why, most of us still use our
   fingers!
       —Bert Kruse.

Computer Eyes
The computer has come of
   age
And is said to be a modern
   sage.
It promises to cure all man's
   ills,
But shows me behind in my
   bills.
It guarantees to cut every
   price
But always charges me twice.
How I eye with mortal terror
This eliminator of human
   error!
       —Mark Deering.

You're Ruining My Credit!
Dear Computer, take a look
   now;
Rally round your balance
   book now.
Try to find my recent
   payment,
On the thirty-first of May
   sent.

I recall it very clearly,
Twenty-seven-fifty merely.
I've received your dunning
   letters;
What a way to treat your
   betters.

Though I know you're trained
   to figure,
My account needs something
   bigger.
So, Computer, try to feed it
To a human who can read it.
       —Peggy McGettigan.

They'll Swallow Anything
   [*"Crumbs from snacks
eaten by programmers are
attracted by electrical charge
on computer tape and cause
errors in the machines."—WSJ
item.*]
The chap who works
   computers
Should get this through his
   "bean":
He must not even nibble
While feeding the machine.
The experts have concluded
There isn't any question

But that a single crumb can
   cause
Computer indigestion.
       —A. S. Flaumenhaft.

Machine Marvel
   Much to the relief of
office workers, the master-
minds have invented a
computer that's so human, on
Monday mornings it comes in
late!
       —Bob Orben.

Calculated Affront
Computers do much of my
   heaviest thinking;
Without them my brain would
   be wearier.
But I hate computers, at this
   there's no blinking,
Because they make me feel
   inferior.
       —Lester A. Sobel.

Suspense Mounting!
It is now your turn;
The others are up and away.
It will take but a moment,
Yet it seems like a day.
Your jaw is set, the step
Is measured,
On your toes, eyes alert,
A slight shift in weight—
All set for the spurt.
Your breathing suspends, a
Functionless respirator,
Now—now—do it!
Ah, you're on the escalator!
       —Arnold J. Zarett.

The Computer—and other Infernal Machines

"If there's anything to evolution, thousands of years from now people will all have bent toes."

Turnstile Turnabout

I don't mind the click it gives
    me
To count me, if it's
    concerned;
What hurts is the kick it gives
    me
As soon as my back is
    turned.
          —Loyd Rosenfield.

Carbonated

No, I haven't been changing
    the oil in the car,
And I haven't been digging a
    hole.
And these smudges you see
    on my fingers and cheeks
Aren't because I've been
    mining for coal.
I am not making up for a
    part in a play
As a dark-faced and
    mischievous gibbon;
These smears that I wear are
    simply because
I've been changing my
    typewriter ribbon!
          —C. M. Bryant.

Sa-tell-ite

Over this thought for
    whatever it's worth,
Maybe we ought to mull:
How much faster ideas
    encircle the earth
Than they penetrate the skull!
          —Thomas Usk.

The Computer—and other Infernal Machines

Ma Bell Beef
The perversity of phones
Throws me in a tizzy!
How come wrong numbers
Never are busy?
   —Ruth M. Walsh.

Problem Punches
I've a question for computer
 types,
Those automated souls:
How can one endorse a
 check
Punched full of holes?
   —Darrell Bartee.

Computer Gap
I write my name with
 hesitation,
As though I have something
 to fear,
But it's not fright nor
 meditation—
Just little holes where it says:
 "Sign Here."
   —Arnold J. Zarett.

Shelley's Shade Dwelling Near A Jetport
Hail to thee, O cacophonous
 carrier,
Bird thou never wert!
Disdainer of a displaced
 wraith,
Dost know or care how my
 ears hurt?
How they throb and nearly
 split asunder
Hourly at thy lockheedless
 thunder?

Thou like a blundering blunt
 scythe
Sliceth through my poor
 personic-barrier
Till I lie limp, unlike myself,
 inert.
Bird or spirit thou damsure
 never wert.
Never. No, nor blithe!
   —E. O. Staley.

This Day and Age
The marvels of modern technology include the development of a soda can which, when discarded, will last forever—and a seven-thousand-dollar car which, when properly cared for, will rust out in two or three years.
   —Paul Harwitz.

With Total Doubt
I have an electric calculator
With which I can swiftly add,
And this should save me a
 lot of time
But doesn't, which makes me
 sad.

You see, every time when
 I've added up
A column of figures long
I add them again, the old-
 fashioned way,
In case the machine is wrong.
   —Richard Armour.

Set for Revenge
I have a new ambition in life
One worthy of my labors.
I'm designing a TV that will
 interfere
With power tools run by my
 neighbors.
   —R. M. Walsh.

Dun For
The computer is like
Some people, I find—
So hard to change once
It makes up its mind.
   —Arnold J. Zarett.

Candid Comment
We have always disparaged the great among us. A lot of people, for example, were pretty sure the inventor of the zipper didn't have all his buttons.
   —Franklin P. Jones.

Person-to-Person
Listen, Alexander Bell,
In bygone days your 'phone
 was swell,
You brought together girls
 and boys
And kids and grandmas, voice
 to voice.
But now recorded messages
 and beeps
Give people everywhere the
 creeps.
Why can't you re-invent the
 'phone?
(Don't answer 'til you hear
 the tone!)
   —Warren Knox.

The Computer—and...

Office Politics

Hooked
The computer is awesome
In the knowledge it stores,
In the facts and figures
It readily outpours.

It demands no pay raise,
Nor sign of affection;
It takes no days off,
Nor time for reflection.

It craves no coffee breaks,
A human eccentricity;
All it ever asks for
Is a little electricity.
                    —Arnold J. Zarett.

Deep Seated Truth
Though the salesman called it
     an "easy" chair,
It's a term that I'm rather in
     doubt of—
It's always the hardest one in
     the house
To get either in to or out of.
                    —E. V. Girand.

Multiple Neurosis
Our civilization's not apt to
     fall
To barbarians at the gate;
We're more likely to drown
     in a tidal wave
Of the letters we duplicate.
                    —G. O. Ludcke.

"This is J. Harley Wainwright, and I want to
speak with whomever the buck stops at."

Office Politics

Business Vocabulary (Translated)

Direct your resources. (Find someone to do it.)

This action is of the highest priority. (I promised the boss.)

Provide an interim reply. (Get them off my back.)

Returned without action. (I don't want it in my files, either.)

Action is being taken. (I'll start it first thing in the morning.)

—Herm Albright.

Counter-Quote

"To thine own self be true"
Doesn't work in the business-
world scrimmage;
For if you do, you probably won't
Fit the corporate image!
—Ruth M. Walsh.

Selective Viewing

The "look at the facts" pitch
Is proper and fine,
Except for one question: which—
Your set or mine?
—Paul Armstrong.

Bitter Truths

Some people know a lot more than they tell. Unfortunately, the reverse is also true.
—Edward Stevenson.

Anybody who says he agrees with you in principle is probably preparing to tell you how wrong you are.
—Franklin P. Jones.

Daffynition

Verbal sniping: the berating game.

Plain Talk

When the meeting agenda
includes this phrase:
"Alternate options are
unclear,"
Translated, the fancy words
simply mean:
"Where do we go from
here?"
—George O. Ludcke.

Success Formula

A self-made successful man told his son, "It's important to keep your feet on the ground; but not always on the same spot."
—Kay Gonovich.

Cliche Corner

Success is never final—and failure never fatal.

Wisdom of the Deep

"Remember," the mama whale instructed the baby whale, "it's only when you get to the top and start blowing off steam that people begin throwing harpoons at you."

"Frankly Speaking"

This beginning means you've
got
For me an earnest earful,
That whether it is frank or
not,
It's sure to be uncheerful.
—Sheldon White.

Lifesmanship Lesson

The best rule of thumb for character is to remember that if you can't be big, don't belittle.
—Dana Robbins.

Planning Ahead

Be nice to co-workers—
Don't be rude, surly, cross;
For you never know when
One may end up your boss.
—G. Sterling Leiby.

Information Pause

A committee is a group of people who usually meet to postpone making a decision.
—Franklin P. Jones.

A good supervisor is one who can coax average people into doing superior work.
—Walter Antoine.

Office Politics

In Conclusion
Few people know how to hold a meeting. Even fewer know how to let it go.
—Robert Fuoss.

Limited Opportunity
I've read up on succeeding
   through self-assertion,
But employing it I'm at a
   loss,
For lately the same books, it
   seems,
Are being read by my boss.
—Edward F. Dempsey.

Executive Talent
If there's an important job to
   be done
And you want to get right to
   it,
Give it to a busy man, who'll
   have
His secretary do it.
—George O. Ludcke.

A Shirt Tale
He has news he wants to
   tell,
But I'm inclined to believe,
When he says it's "off the
   cuff,"
He has something up his
   sleeve.
—Rosemarie Williamson.

Subtlebutt
Sticks and stones may break
   your bones,

Some speeches are laced with
   invective;
Direct charges abound,
While others have found
Innuendoes are more effective.
—Gail Cooke.

Indispensable
An employe who survived all sorts of personnel turnovers and purges at his company was asked the secret of his survival.

"Oh, they don't dare fire me," he replied. "I'm always too far behind in my work."
—Edward Stevenson.

Jargon Jitters
Please, give me no
   "directives"—
I am tired of the term.
Nor do I want your
   "guidelines";
Just the mention makes me
   squirm.
I won't contribute "input,"
(Though I'll gladly have my
   say);
If you ask me to
   "communicate,"
My answer's, "Not today."
I'm dead set against "relating"
(But I'll be a loyal friend);
And, if you ask for this "in
   depth,"
Forget it. It's the end.
—Marie Daerr Boehringer.

Grim Factor
If a man can smile while everything is going wrong at the office it's probably because he has already lined up another job.
—Robert Fuoss.

Mixed Opinion
It's surprising how marks can
   vary on
An executive's on-the-job
   rating;
His boosters describe him as
   "flexible"—
His critics say he's
   "vacillating."
—George O. Ludcke.

Loophole
"Does the new company rule about officers not employing their relatives mean that I can't be your executive assistant any more, Dad?" the president's son asked.

"Nonsense, my boy!" his father replied. "I'll get around that by disowning you!"
—Edward Stevenson.

A Simple Plea
If at first you do succeed, try, try not to be insufferable.
—Franklin P. Jones.

Fitness Report
"What makes you think your job is shaky?" a young

Office Politics

wife asked. "I thought they just put your name on the door."

"They did," moaned her husband. "In pencil!"
—Robert Fuoss.

Time Out!
At a meeting or private brawl
I never get flustered at all
At some loaded question or
    directive,
As I have a defense that's
    effective.
For, when the full meaning I
    can seize,
I say, "Repeat the question,
    please!"
And, though the speaker's
    voice is quite clear,
I shout, "Louder! I can't
    hear!"
And the one that I have
    down pat
Is, "Would you care to
    rephrase that?"
Or, if my opponent's real
    tough, I'll state,
"Would you like to
    elaborate?"
For I find that it always pays
To use the above cliches
As they allow me time to try
To think up a good reply.
—Leonard Dittell.

Women's Rights—and Lefts

Women's Rights—and Lefts

Bus Ride
I view liberation's delights
With a disenchanted frown—
Since women stood up for
   their rights,
We're doing much less sitting
   down.
                —May Richstone.

Women's Lib
Though men may make the
   greater fuss
About how they're
   polygamous
The same sauce serves for
   goose as gander:
We women like to polyander.
                —Ruth Boorstin.

Sauce for the Gander
   Equality of the sexes
cannot really be said to have
arrived until a few young
husbands get mad and go
home to dad.
                —Robert Fuoss.

Blow-Up
   [*"New in stores: An
inflatable man-like figure to
accompany women driving
alone at night."—WSJ Briefs.*]
A spinster whose firm
   ultimatum
On men was, "I won't
   tolerate 'em"
Nonetheless bought platoons
Of these man-like balloons,
Explaining, "I love to deflate
   'em!"
                —E. V. Girand.

What Price Glory?
Armed with a B.S. degree
And ready to set the world
   aflame
With enumerations of science
   honors,
And accolades of campus
   fame,
I met the corporation man
Who seemed to have but one
   gripe:
He nodded with unimpressed
   reserve and said,
"That's nice, but can you
   type?"
                —M. Catherine Driscoll.

Just Waiting, Thanks
With all my heart I pay this
   trib
To those who fight for
   Women's Lib:
I marvel as they smash the
   chains
That bar them from the male
   domains,
And cheer with long and wild
   applause
Their speeches on their
   worthy cause.
I view their marches, sing
   their songs,
And vow to help them right
   their wrongs.

I trust, however, when they've
   won
The rights that men have,
   one by one,
And take with pride their
   rightful place

As equals in our human race,
Their true nobility will then
Assert itself and once again
They'll start, as only they are
   able,
To get the supper on the
   table.
                —D. N. McKay.

Epitaph
On Monday she had bowling,
On Tuesday, PTA
On Wednesday it was bridge
   club
That occupied her day.
Sorority on Thursday,
On Friday, Ladies' Aid;
Committees filled her week-
   ends,
But she was not dismayed.
Her civic groups and hobbies
Required her every breath:
Here lies a modern woman
Who, alas, was clubbed to
   death!
                —Ellie Womack.

Fem-Lib Ceres
   [*"We probably ought to
have a woman as Secretary
of Agriculture—the old
mythology didn't have a god
of agriculture, it was just a
goddess."—Notable &
Quotable*].
What do you mean, sir, "just
   a goddess"?
She of the draped and
   buxom bodice.
She whose power guarantees

Women's Rights—and Lefts

Bounty from the fields and
   trees
Is "just a goddess"? She can
   call
The sun to shine, the rain to
   fall.
You'd imply she's lesser than
A god? Why, sir, he's just a
   man!
                —E. V. Girand.

On Shaky Ground
When it comes to equal
   rights,
A few demands I greet with
   mirth;
They tell me there's now a
   group
That's advocating "Father
   Earth."
        —Rosemarie Williamson.

It's About Time!
That a woman's place is in
   the house
Has long been a masculine
   tenet.
I'll go along with it, with the
   stipulation
That it's also in the Senate.
                —R. M. Walsh.

Equal Footing
Few are the men who now
   rise to their feet
To gallantly offer a lady a
   seat;
They're fast disappearing,
   these chivalrous knights,

While women are left
   standing up for their rights!
                —Charlotte Koss.

Lib Fib
As a liberated fem, I detest
   flattery.
And I tell men so, looking
   them
Straight in the eye.
But deep in my heart, I
   know darn well
That I lie.
                —R. M. Walsh.

Work's Climax
Monday I march against
   busing,
Tuesday I protest for peace,
Wednesday the grape
   demonstration,
Thursday the sit-in for Greece.
Friday I lead the smog rally,
Saturday's march is on crime;
Sunday my family riots
For silly old meals served on
   time!
                —B. C. Boyd.

In Hot Water
   We can't believe equality
between the sexes can exist
until a man is interviewed on
the TV commercials about his
dishpan hands.
                —Gil Stern.

Lib-Lorn
The impact of Women's Lib
Is affecting romantic hours.
In proposing, instead of
   "Please be mine,"
The suitor says, "Let's be
   ours."
                —R. M. Walsh.

Semi-Liberated
She doesn't want me helping
   her,
By holding her coat or chair,
And opening a door for her
Will get me an icy glare.

She thinks my courtly
   manners
To be old-fashioned as heck,
But she makes one bow to
   tradition
By letting me pick up the
   check.
                —Edward F. Dempsey.

Littlest Libber
Said the little girl in the toy
   store,
Pushing aside the alphabet
   blocks,
"I don't see why you don't
   carry
A simple Jill-in-the-Box!"
                —R.M. Walsh.

Short-Order Kook
It's not at serving chops of
   pork
Or lamb that she is tops;
No, this gal's famed for

Women's Rights—and Lefts

dishing out
First-rate karate chops.
   —G. Sterling Leiby.

Thumbs Down
Women's Lib may be fine for
 some,
But some of us see a hiatus
In the whole concept of
 equality—
We prefer our superior status!
   —May Richstone.

Look Again!
Men and Women created
 equal?
They are, and my words are
 authentical.
And yet, and this is my
 sequel,
Equal isn't the same as
 identical.
   —Richard Armour.

Surprise!
Mother's demand for equal
 rights
Threw poor dad for a loss;
He never dreamed through all
 these years
That he had been the boss!
   —Maurice Seitter.

Status Quota
Women are plugging equality,
But what is there to fret
 them?
When it comes to seeking
 men's wages,
Didn't they always get them?
   —G. O. Ludcke.

Something Mizzing
[" 'Ms.' gains as a proper
way to address women."—
WSJ news item.]
Dear feminists, I feel there is
A flaw in that "Ms." (called
 "Miz").
I'll frankly say you're wrong
 to rate us
As glad to cloak our wedded
 status.

With men equality we claim.
Among us girls, it's not the
 same.
If all are "Miz," no Mrs. can
Show misses she has got her
 man!
   —Judy Michaels.

The Worm Turneth
My moustache takes time to
 trim,
The cologne must be just
 right,
My sideburns need careful
 leveling
Before we step out for the
 night.
My coiffure can use some
 teasing

So my curly locks will bounce
 free,
And now that my wife's been
 liberated
Her free time's spent waiting
 for me!
   Arnold J. Zarett.

Vive l'Egalite!
Three cheers for liberation!
Now women, with their
 brawn,
Can change the tires
And put out fires
As well as mow the lawn!
   —S. Omar Barker.

Glib Lib
I hadn't been too informed
 about
The Women's Lib movement,
 per se,
Until a female gas station
 attendant asked,
"Fill him up?" the other day.
   —R. M. Walsh.

New Hobby
All the hours my wife
 devoted
To mah-jong or canasta night
Have been given over
To the liberation fight.
   —Arnold J. Zarett.

Unyielding
In the latest of women's lib
 movements,
One cannot get too far, I

Women's Rights—and Lefts

    fear,
Unless one decides to let go
    of
Her greatest of weapons—the
    tear.
                —Jay Russell.

Lib's Reading List
    With the Women's Lib movement making all those advances, we can expect a new release of many classic plays and books. Such as: "Donna Quixote," "Death of A Saleswoman," "Mrs. Roberts," "Doris Copperfield," "Lady of the Flies," "Dame Lancelot," "Queen Lear" and "The Girl Who Came to Dinner."
                —Herb Gochros.

"I'm sorry, sir. You can't list a blown mind as
a capital loss."

Cornering the Economists

"Gentlemen, next year's model! Much less powerful, much shorter, much lighter, and much more expensive than THIS year's model!

Sixty Percent Chance

If you take a close look at the government's economic predictions you have to wonder if the Weather Bureau hasn't taken over the forecasts.

—Robert Fuoss.

Local Success

Hold down the increase in
the money supply,
Is the economists' constant
plea.
To ease their worries I can
assure them
I's not been increasing near
me.

—Edward F. Dempsey.

Verbal Market

Talk is still cheap. Probably because the supply greatly exceeds the demand.

—Franklin P. Jones.

Academic Credentials

An economist is a person who lectures on capital and labor. And the baffling thing is that most of them qualified for this career by having no capital and having done no labor.

—Robert Fuoss.

Coming to Terms

I remember the good old days

Cornering the Economists

With more than a little clarity,
When an overheated economy
Was known by the term
    "prosperity."
                —Richard Armour.

Economic Doubt Look
Some pundits vow depression
    looms,
While others swear that
    business booms,
And those who have the
    lowdown claim
That soon we'll play the
    slowdown game.
Don't worry if you feel
    perplexed—
The experts can't agree what's
    next!
                —W. J. Cronenberger.

Dim View
Economic forecasters, in my
    esteem,
Rank quite far down the line;
Since they keep their jobs by
    predicting
When I'll be losing mine.
                —Edward F. Dempsey.

Ecology-Economy Note
    Now that we're doing
something about America's
wildlife, can't we start by
preserving nest eggs?

End of Mystery
I figured it out this morning
Just what these words have
    meant:

"Mitchell! I've found two economists that agree!"

Cornering the Economists

In Depressions we're really
    broke—
In Recessions we're merely
    bent.
                    —Robert Orben.

Mixed Meanings:
    Conglomerate: crazy
mixture of dissimilar
businesses.
    Diversified Growth
Company: conglomerate as
described in the annual
report.

Either, or
A good economic forecaster
Is a prognosticator who won't
Hesitate to foretell things that
    will happen
(Or to explain why not, when
    they don't.)
                    —George O. Ludcke.

Cash Course
"The dollar's ill and needs a
    boost,"
A Keynesian might say;
(Just like a sickly patient
Needs vitamins each day.)
The Monetarist says, "We're
    overhot.
The dollar needs a rest;
(Stay in bed, slow down
    some,
It really would be best.)
The answer, though, is some
    of both:
At least that's what I'd do:

Vitamins and rest in bed
The dollar has the flu.
                    —Harry Chernoff.

Down to Earth
Land is a good investment—
Few options rank above it;
Its supply is fixed and the
    government
Hasn't learned how to print
    more of it.
                    —George O. Ludcke.

Self-Defeating
The economic expert
Who helps devise a plan
To reduce mass
    unemployment
Must be a troubled man;
He's got his job cut out for
    him
From which he cannot shirk
Until employment rises—
And then he's out of work!
                    —Charlotte Koss.

Realistic Approach
    Isn't it about time
Washington dropped that
outmoded index and switched
to a Cost of Living Altimeter?
                    —Edward Stevenson.

Daffynition
    Recession: lapse of luxury.
                    —Lane Olinghouse.

Taxes—
Holes and Loopholes

Skinned Specimens
The difference between a tax
    collector
And a taxidermist is the fact
That the taxidermist leaves
The hide intact.
                    —R. M. Walsh.

Breaking Point
Taxes are so much of our
    paycheck
With the promise of more to
    come,
It makes one think we're
    approaching
A total eclipse of the sum.
                    —Edward F. Dempsey.

Time Bomb
    No rest for the taxpayer!
Now that we've finished
educating the World War II
babies, it's time to build
nursing homes for the babies
of World War I.
                    —Robert Fuoss.

Blanket Deposit
Protection against all
    contingencies
From the cradle to the grave
Is a very comforting goal for
    which
All of us should save.
But before we turn over our
    pay check
And ask Uncle Sam to bank
    it,

Taxes—Holes and Loopholes

"Relax—it stands for 'Island Rescue Service.'"

We should figure the cost in
   Taxes
Of that old Security Blanket.
   —George O. Ludcke.

Arrear Guard Needed
Just when my war on poverty
Gets in a good position,
Somebody sneaks up back of
   me
And swipes my ammunition.
   —S. S. Biddle.

Ode to Conservationists
Concerning our natural
   resources,
We'd better prepare for the
   worst.
Of those that will soon be
   exhausted
The taxpayer may be the
   first.
   —Mildred N. Hoyer.

Daffynitions
   Inheritance taxes: Shear
the-wealth program.
   —Raymond J. Cvikota.

   Social Security: slaving
grace.
   —Daisy Brown.

   Income tax: The hauls of
Congress.
   —Tom McElwee.

Taxes—Holes and Loopholes

For Keeps
I keep receipts,
I keep them all,
I do not thin or weed them.
I keep receipts
With care until
The day before I need them.
　　　　　—Richard Armour.

Morality Tale
Recently, the IRS received a letter from an anonymous taxpayer stating that he had cheated on income tax, and his conscience was bothering him to such an extent that he couldn't sleep. The letter concluded: "I'm enclosing $50 —and if I still can't sleep, I'll send the balance."
　　　　　—Doris Dolphin.

Candid Comments
If the good Lord meant us to pay income tax, He'd have made us smart enough to prepare the return.
　　　　　—Franklin P. Jones.

Tax loopholes are like parking spaces; they disappear just when you get there.

Financial Secrets
Though having "untold
　　wealth"
Is considered a mark of
　　success,

It sure can cause you trouble
With the IRS!
　　　　　—Mary Lee Sauermann.

Non-Shining Example
["*Cost estimates for the missile-firing submarine Trident were censored out of the public transcript.*"—News Item]
Next year I'll be much richer.
I'll have some cash to burn.
I'll print "This sum is
　　censored"
Acorss my tax return.
　　　　　—Ramona Demery.

Salary Stalk
A friend of ours says he could live on what he makes if he could get his hands on it.
　　　　　—Bill Copeland.

Federal Payroll
People who sneer at bureaucrats should remember that all of us work for the government. A bureaucrat gets paid for it.
　　　　　—Robert Fuoss.

Advice
Here's an admonition
That I believe
A truth that's indestructible;
"It's more blessed to give
Than to receive"—
And it's deductible
　　　　　—Ruth Boorstin.

House Recalls
These days, the way spiraling taxes are causing widespread loss of homes, it's small wonder we're hearing so much of property rites.
　　　　　—Bert Murray.

On Second Thought
It must be nice to be rich
And deal in gigantic sums;
But remember, the more you
　　make,
The more taxing life becomes.
　　　　　—Herm Albright.

Self Employed
Though others tax my
　　earnings with
The greatest assiduity,
To find deductions, I myself
Must tax my ingenuity.
　　　　　—Richard Armour.

Dead Letter Department
A Kansas City, Mo., tax collector received the following letter: "As I have notified your office before, I have been deceased since 1965. Please remove my name from the tax rolls."
　　　　　—Harold Helfer.

Crime Doesn't Pay
Income tax: Fine you pay for reckless thriving.

Taxes—Holes and Loopholes

Taxes
Just like the fighting
    champions
When slugging for the crown:
Although they may be
    staggering,
They seldom do go down!
          —Helen G. Sutin.

Progress?
An old timer is a person
whose annual property tax
now exceeds what he paid
for the place originally.

Dirge for April Fifteenth
Prosperity is something that
    you feel;
You greet it with a rapturous
    caress;
And after that affectionate
    reception,
You fold and mail it quickly
    to the IRS!
          —Bob Herz.

Tax Facts
This time of year we all are
    ill-fated
And must file tax forms so
    complicated
That only the brightest can
    ferret out
The correct method of filling
    them out;
The apparent fact that seems
    almost funny:
Tax filing is as hard as
    making money.
          —Colleen Stanley Bare.

Charge It
Taxes, taxes, again they are
    due,
To make us worry and fret
    and stew,
Wondering how we're going
    to pay them
And if, somehow, we could
    delay them,
When truly the answer isn't
    hard:
We just need a U.S.
    Taxacard!
          —Colleen Stanley Bare.

Tax Return
Divide line two by three,
Enter result on four.
Add line five or six,
Whichever is more.

Instructions like these,
On pages three to eight,
Contribute to the feeling
This filing may be late.
          —Darrell Bartee.

Over and Over
They say he overtaxed
    himself,
A foolish thing to say.
It was the government, of
    course,
Or else his CPA.

Perhaps he undertaxed
    himself,
But I would not applaud it,
At least not till three years
    have passed
And he's not had an audit.
          —Richard Armour.

Tax Trap
For those inclined to play
It fast and loose,
Sometimes a tax loophole
Ends up a noose.
          —Robert Wallace.

Government Issue
Internal Revenue, by
popular demand, has come
up with a simplified tax
return form, effective next
year:

(a) How much did you make
in wages or commissions after
deductions?
(b) How much did you make
    on horse races or bingo or
    like that?
(c) Total (a) and (b)
(d) How much have you got
    left?
(e) How much more can you
    borrow?
(f) Total (d) and (e), add
    10%, and send it in.
          —William Lodge.

Form Feeling
They've changed the rules on
    income tax,
A fact that makes me burn.
I think perhaps that I have
    reached
The point of no return!
          —Dick Emmons.

Taxes— Holes and Loopholes

The Stock Market

Dollar Dolor

We disapprove of government
　spending,
Deplore the cost of all that
　lending,
Decry the interest rate until
We want to buy a Treasury
　Bill.
　　　　—Mary Ellen Donner.

Suggestion Box

Our states have had a
"Use" tax for many years. We
now suggest a "What's the
use" tax.
　　　　—Raymond J. Cvikota.

Inside Job

Burglars are dumb. Here
they are still heisting payrolls
when everybody knows the
real dough is in the
deductions.
　　　　—Robert Fuoss.

Incomplete Sound Track

The two Voyager probes
that departed Cape Canaveral
toward Jupiter and Saturn
carried recordings of typical
earth sounds; dogs barking,
cows mooing and birds
chirping. Apparently nobody
thought of taxpayers
screaming.
　　　　—Franklin P. Jones.

"It's Mrs. Hawthorne. She wants to know
what sirloin opened at today."

The Stock Market

Wall Street Revisited
[*Reprinted by special request.*
In keeping with the nostalgia
trend.]
I possess a strong affinity
For the street that's topped
   by Trinity,
And pleasant feelings e'er
   ensue
Each time I stroll through
   Wall past New;
Indeed, my bliss doth wax
   intense
At Broad and Nassau's
   confluence,
While just a glimpse of
   William Street
Beguiles me into raptures
   sweet!
Gosh, how my cup of joy
   ran over
When first espying quaint
   Hanover.
Now, eastward-ho to lovely
   Pearl
And Water, with my head
   awhirl,
Then sprightly Front and
   spacious South,
Abutting the East River's
   mouth!
To some, the Street connotes
   finance—
To me, though, it's my Big
   Romance!
       —Sally Ann McCarthy.

Fowl Ball
I'm a stockmarket player who
   declares

With stock market jitters I'm
   stricken,
I do not run with the bulls
   and bears.
As a matter of fact I'm
   chicken.
       —Georgie Starbuck Galbraith.

Contrarian
When most of the analysts
   tell me to buy,
I hurriedly sell and go short.
And when they get worried
   and urge me to sell,
"Let's buy!" is my ready
   retort.

By using this method in trade
   after trade
I've managed in most every
   one
To make sure my profits are
   always cut short,
While letting my losses all
   run.
       —Joseph P. Waitz.

Hunter's Return
Stalking the market
In good times or ill
Limits choices, but I'm sure I
   'druther
Be chasing a bull
Up one side of the hill
Than a bear chasing me
   down the other.
       —Warren Knox.

Faint Praise
I know that my stock market
   playing friend
Has lost on another caper
When he trumpets, "I hit the
   jackpot,"
Then adds, in a whisper, "On
   paper."
       —George O. Ludcke.

Snicker Tape
Friends often snicker at my
   investments,
And it sends me into shock,
When an issue I've carefully
   researched
Ends up as a laughing stock.
       —Edward F. Dempsey.

Discriminatory
[*"One Group That Should*
Not Buy Any Stocks, A New
Theory Suggests, Is the
Stockbroker."—WSJ headline].
This suggestion's unfair
And should, of course, be
   spurned;
Brokers have every right
To also get burned.
       —Arnold J. Zarett.

Livestock
People who complain about
The stock market to their
   peers,
Usually cite the bulls and the
   bears
When they should blame the
   bum steers!
       —R. M. Walsh.

The Stock Market

Facts of Life
A father's work is never done
When he's entrusted with a
    son.
He's scarce explained the
    birds and bees,
To sonny sitting at his knees,
When he is faced with
    greater cares:
He must explain the bulls
    and bears.
                —Ellie Womack.

The Bullish Bear
When the markt's trend is
    clouded
By obscurities,
My small portfolio is filled
    with
Insecurities.
            —Lenore Eversole Fisher.

Bear's Eye
The market has made its
    move,
It is out of its mire.
Blue chips and glamors are
    strong,
They move higher and higher,
My holdings I view with
    delight
Rising smartly from where
    they sat.
Up, up, way up they shoot
Straight to what I bought
    them at.
                —Arnold J. Zarett.

Gym Dandy
Give me a stock that's active,
That jumps and never quits,
That soars with grace
    attractive,
And winds up doing splits!
                —Bert Kruse.

Master Investor
He sits behind the desk and
    frowns
Upon the market's ups and
    downs.
In this stock low, or is it
    high?
Should he sell now, or
    should he buy?
To buy? To sell? Which is
    the wiser?
He must consult his staunch
    adviser—
So, wasting no more precious
    time
In pondering, he flips a dime.
                —G. Sterling Leiby.

Warning
There's a world of difference
    between
(And this should be
    understood)
A good, sound investment
And an investment that
    sounds good!
                —Ruth M. Walsh.

Emphatic Equivocations
"The market's bound to rise
    . . . unless
It goes down . . . which it
    might
If bonds become more
    attractive
And interest rates go out of
    sight."
"This could, of course, be the
    time to sell . . ."
Some advisers suggest that
    path,
"But if you decide to plunge
    now,
You may end up taking a
    bath."
It's great to have learned
    counsel
To consult before you try it . . .
For any action, at any time,
Someone will justify it.
                —George O. Ludcke.

Stocking Up
Some stocks have income,
    some have growth,
But what I seek are stocks
    with both.
The stocks for which I yearn
    and chafe
Are speculative, also safe.
I like a stock that booms in
    war
And yet in peace does better
    far,
A company of large small
    size,

The Stock Market

With management that's
   young but wise.
What motivates me, shapes
   each deed,
Each waking thought and
   impulse? Greed!
                  —Richard Armour.

Pfd. Position
Quite frequently, when stocks
   go down
And leave me inward
   quaking,
The analysts attribute it
To what's called "profit
   taking."
I have an argument with this,
And here's what's at the
   heart of it;
When profit's being taken, I
Don't seem to be a part of
   it.
                  —Dick Emmons.

Name Tag
   A technical rally is what
your broker calls it when
almost everything else goes
up except the stock he sold
you.
                  —Robert Fuoss.

Feeling Me Out
I feel it in my bones, I say,
But this my dreadful plight is:
Is it a hunch to buy or sell
Or is it just arthritis?
                  —Richard Armour.

Communique From G.H.Q.
There's a martial air to the
   market report
When analysts tell us the
   answers
Why "stocks retreat on a
   wide front" and
"Casualties outnumber
   advancers."
                  —George O. Ludcke.

Market Margin
I lost a fortune in the market,
The details would only bore;
To put it concisely, my
   shopping bag
Broke in the grocery store.
                  —Ruth M. Walsh.

Daffynitions
Optimist: a hope addict.
                  —Honey Greer.

   Dreamer: A person who
jumps to illusions.
                  —Maurice Seittler.

New Twist
I used to study the earnings
Of a stock before I'd buy;
I'd carefully chart the rhythm
Of its swings to low and
   high;

I'd analyze the management
To see how the stock did
   rate,
But now I just ask whether
It's a takeover candidate.
                  —Arnold J. Zarett.

Street Scene
   One investor to another;
"No sense of humor? So
what are you doing in the
market?"
                  —M. D. Reay.

Troika
"Stock averages will fall,"
Some experts advise,
While others scoff and state:
"There'll be a further rise."

But I've a third view,
I do have to say;
My statistics show
It could go either way.
                  —Arnold J. Zarett.

The Investor
Business and financial news
Is all I ever read.
I've droppd my other hobbies,
I'm tied in now to greed.
With Mr. Dow and Mr. Jones
My days begin and end.
I'm constantly tuned in
To the latest Wall Street
   trend.
I worry about my investment,
I dream of bulls and bears.
I haven't had a peaceful
   moment
Since I purchased those two
   shares.
                  —Ann Wells.

The Stock Market

Hedge'Opting

When you make a "Put,"
 you're betting
That the price of the stock
 will fall;
But you hope it goes up
 (and the higher, the better)
In case you've placed a
 "Call."

And when you're involved in
 a "Straddle,"
(In case you've decided to rig
 one)
You don't care if the price
 goes up or down,
Just so the change is a big
 one!

—George O. Ludcke.

Arkeologist

As a financier, old Noah
Was vastly underrated—
He floated his stock, when
 everyone else
Was being liquidated.

—G.O. Ludcke.

Define Your Terms

Business terms can be
 confusing
And their meanings just a bit
 flaky;
A lightly-held company can
 be firm,
But somtimes a firm can be
 shaky.

—G. O. Ludcke.

The Stock Market

Back Track
Charting the daily market
   reports
Keeps track of what shape
   stocks are in;
It doesn't tell where they're
   going,
But it's nice to know where
   they've been.
              —G.O. Ludcke.

Expertease
A hard one for brokers to
   answer
When they're making a sales
   pitch:
"If you're such a stock
   market expert,
How come you're not rich?"
              —G.O. Ludcke.

Wouldn't You Know It?
The day after I buy—
"The market's abrupt
downturn was regarded as an
overdue technical correction
following the recent prolonged
run-up."
The day after I sell—
"The long-awaited up-swing in
prices came as no surprise to
Wall Street observers who
noted that the long sell-off
period was bound to reverse
itself."
          —George O. Ludcke.

Broker-ese
"Just profit taking," brokers
   say.
As market turns and tosses.
It's seldom put the other way:
"Just people taking losses."
             —W. D. Hayes.

Economic Lesson
   The senior financial analyst
for a large brokerage house
had the first dollar he ever
earned hanging above his
desk in a 10¢ wooden frame.
   A new junior employe said,
"Interesting. The dollar is now
worth 10¢—the frame $1."
   The analyst replied, "But
my total investment is still
worth its cost."
   Said his younger co-worker,
"But if you had put the
dollar in a savings bank at
4%, 40 years ago, drawn the
interest, you would still have
the original investment, plus
$1.60 to spend or reinvest."
   Whereupon the senior
analyst resigned.

Inflation

Dated Law
In school we were taught
About supply and demand,
An economic law
Not hard to understand.
But what we learned then
No longer applies,
Because no matter what—
The prices just rise.
          —Arnold J. Zarett.

Up and Up
Our incomes rise from year
   to year.
But no need for elation
When we find out how much
   is real
And how much is inflation.
          —G. Sterling Leiby.

On the Level
   Inflation has bestowed
upon the United States total
democracy: for the first time
in human history, luxuries and
necessities cost exactly the
same.
          —Paul Harwitz.

Absorbing Food Prices
First the price of sugar rose,
Then coffee followed suit,
Lettuce prices soared and
   thus
Became forbidden fruit.
Fish is out of sight in cost;
Meat prices aren't funny.
I think the cheapest way to
   thrive
Would be to eat our money!
          —Sima Pomerantz.

Inflation

"I'll have to re-check these items. You've got the price stickers all tear stained."

Balancing Out

As prices rise
Past contemplation,
I keep calm
Amidst inflation.
My step stays firm,
My smile is beaming—
Of course, at night
I wake up screaming.
—Robert Gordon.

Daffynitions

Food budgeting: shelf denial.
—Daisy Brown.

Inflation: When your child gets his first job at a salary you dreamed of as the culmination of your career.
—Paul Harwitz.

Utility increases: the old rate race.
—Herm Albright.

Beef Price Personal

For Sale: Complete set of steak knives, like new, used once in 1969.
—Gertrude Pierson.

Shear Irony

Just about the time you think you've found a hedge against inflation, someone clips it.
—Bill Copeland.

Inflation

Good as Gold
Nowadays if you want to teach a child the value of a dollar, you had better be quick about it.
—Duane Dewlap.

Cancellation
If money is the means to an end, then inflation is an end to the means.
—Maurice Seitter.

Economy Note
With the high cost of living these days, it's cheaper by the doesn't.
—Selma Glasser.

Change of Pace
Turnpike travel is expensive.
It's strictly pay as you go.
I know because my quarters
And dollars have tolled me so!
—Jean Conder Soule.

Small Change
According to the lore we learned,
A penny saved is a penny earned.
But times have changed, and now I'm thinking:
A penny saved is a penny shrinking.
—Diantha Warfel.

Discriminating Errand Man
A woman called her husband at his office to ask if he would have time to stop at the cleaners on his way home. He replied, "That depends—on whether you mean the laundry or the supermarket."
—Lane Olinghouse.

Dior Jam
You know inflation's here to stay,
Leastwise for the present,
When it takes a hundred bucks or more
To dress up like a peasant!
—Charlotte Koss.

A Touch of Class
Noticing the menu of a seafood restaurant listed lobster at $17.85, a diner asked the waiter, "What comes with this item?"
The waiter shrugged and replied, "The apologies of the manager."
—Lane Olinghouse.

Tilt
This is how
The economy's bent:
My utilities now
Exceed my rent.
—Arnold J. Zarett.

State of the Nation
Two questions keep driving me almost insane.
They furrow my brow with care:
Will we ever get back to normal again?
Or are we already there?
—S. Omar Barker.

Inflation Rate
Everything continues to go up. Now, it's rumored, you have to give four cheers for the Red, White and Blue.
—Robert Fuoss.

Disappointed Rounds
There is only one sure way to slow down inflation. Turn it over to the Post Office.
—Bob Orben.

Choice Cut
I'm glad when hearing from the banks,
That the prime rate's taking a drop,
But I'd rejoice much more on hearing it,
From my local butcher shop.
—Edward F. Dempsey.

Too Far?
It's time to cut expenses—
Goodbye, ties made of silk;
Farewell, filets and frog legs

Inflation

And goodies of that ilk. . . .
I've even thought of switching
From shaving cream to milk.
　　　　　—G. Sterling Leiby.

Upgraded
　　Most of us are living in a
more expensive neighborhood
now, and we didn't even
have to move.
　　　　　—Lucille S. Harper.

Turnabout
I was once an impulse
　　shopper,
A fact now hard to believe;
These days I look at prices
And my impulse is to leave.
　　　　　—Mini Kay.

Dollar Signs

"My God, I can get a better interest rate than
that from the *Mob!*"

Dollar Signs

Line on the Cash
Money isn't everything; but make a lot of it before you start talking such nonsense!
—Paul Harwitz.

Forgive Us Our Debts
Credit card buying comes
  naturally,
As charge-plans become more
  vast;
Most people are accustomed
  to
Paying now for sins of the
  past.
—R. M. Walsh.

Daffynitions
Refinancing: debt warmed over.

Roster of charitable donors; succor list.
—Robert Fuoss.

Bankruptcy: after all is sad and dun.

Hoarded money: Cache transaction.
—Raymond J. Cvikota.

Candid Comment
We may never succeed in curing poverty—but with prices and taxes they way they are, we're going to cure wealth.
—Lucille S. Harper.

Cash And Carry
Nobody can fix things around the house better than the man who's handy with a checkbook.

Middle Ground
People say it's better to be poor and happy than rich and miserable, but couldn't someone work something out, such as being moderately wealthy and merely moody?
—Paul Harwitz.

Get The Point?
A mark almost infinitesimal,
And yet important, is the
  decimal.
A little move to left or right
And sums drop low or reach
  new height.
The decimal is just a dot,
Yet where it is can mean a
  lot.
—Richard Armour.

Economy Note
One good thing about those new two-dollar bills— they should help us cut down on our buck-passing.
—Herm Albright.

The Other Half's View
I do not lie awake at night
Nor let it spoil my appetite.
Nor have I wasted precious
  years
In weeping foolish, idle tears
And fussing in dismay about
The things I have to do
  without.
Us poorer folks appreciate
What we do have. I think it's
  great,
And those with money, I am
  sure
Have many problems to
  endure,
And being rich won't put an
  end
To trouble—nor does money
  mend,
It's just that being rich, for
  me,
Would add style to my
  misery!
—Alison Wyrley Birch.

Dim View
A man with an overdue bill received this note from the power company: "We would be delighted if you would pay your bill. You will be delighted if you don't."
—Herm Albright.

On Borrowed Time
"Floating a loan" is a
  pleasant sound
For something I simply don't
  hanker,
Such a bouncy, buoyant
  phrase
For what often seems like an
  anchor!
—Arnold J. Zarett.

Dollar Signs

Old Masters Preferred
[*"—designs and sells personalized checks decorated with a sketch of the customer, a business trademark, and checks in odd colors."—WSJ Business Bulletin.*]
I'll gladly take checks that are arty,
In colors the wildest extant,
If they can be swapped for engravings
Of Hamilton, Jackson or Grant!
—E. V. Girand.

Trust Fun
A businessman visited his banker and asked, "Are you worried about whether I can meet my note next month?"
"Frankly, I am," confessed the banker.
"Good," replied the client. "That's what I pay you 12 percent for."
—Herm Albright.

Down Under
Credit is a device,
No matter your plan or goal,
That lets you start at the bottom
And go in the hole!
—Ruth M. Walsh.

Easy Road to Wealth
Follow this advice, and trust,
And you will thrive from small beginning:
Never bet, but if you must,
Bet only with your winnings.
—William Walden.

First Come, First Served
My car has been recalled by the plant.
I'd like to oblige them, but I can't.
I'll drop them a note why I can't do it:
The finance company beat them to it!
—F. O. Walsh.

Suggested Course
It would be better for our collective morale if people stopped telling us what money can't buy and listed a few things that it can.
—Franklin P. Jones.

Separator
When it comes to telling a quarter and a nickel apart these days, only a vending machine knows for sure.
—Herm Albright.

Blue Period
Few realize the blessing of being poor until they have got over it.
—Lane Olinghouse.

Proper Restraint
If you're trying to hold down your bills,
Here's a method that's found to be great:
There's nothing that actually fills
The need like a good paperweight.
—S. S. Biddle.

For Whom the Bill Tolls
[*"Consumers are finding it increasingly hard to pay their past due bills, the American Collectors Association reports "—WSJ news item.*]
Do not speak harshly of the man
Who cannot pay his bills;
He's only doing what he can
To cure the country's ills.
It's due in part to his neglect
The GNP is buoyed,
For thus the people who collect
These bills remain employed!
—E. V. Girand.

Mostly Honor
Honorarium,
I've come to see,
Is a very big word
For a very small fee.
—Richard Armour

Dollar Signs

Proof Positive
I crave no accolade of fame,
Toward wealth my attitude's
    the same,
Of the simple life I never tire,
This proves I'm wise—also a
    liar!
                        —S. Omar Barker.

Sign Language
Placard on wall of a
highway diner: "Please do not
ask for credit. You knew
yesterday you would have to
eat today."

Financial Witchery
Checkbook in hand, the
man said to the bank teller,
"The balance I have and the
balance in the bank's
statement I've just received
don't agree, and I wonder if
you could help straighten this
out."
"I'll try," said the teller.
"What is your balance?"
"That's not fair!" cried the
man, "I asked you first!"
                        —Harold Helfer.

Timely Truism
"A dollar to a doughnut" we
    used to say,
But now we're in need of a
    sequel;
With the dollar behaving the
    way that it is,
The odds are almost equal.
                        —Amy Vance Weeks.

Texas Revisited
A millionaire oilman went
to his dentist for his six-
month check-up. When the
dentist reported that his teeth
appeared in perfect condition,
the tycoon was disappointed.
"Couldn't you just go
ahead and drill, anyway,
Doc?" he asked, "I feel lucky
today!"
                        —Ola Beavers.

Cash Rehash
"It's only money!"
Some people opine,
Usually when they're
Speaking of mine.
                        —Gail Cooke.

In Flashing Lights Yet
It's too easy to overspend
    these days;
What we need is a credit
    card built
So that when we've exceeded
    our balance
The computer will register
    "Tilt."
                        —George O. Ludcke.

Timely Tidbit
Wealthy people miss one
of life's greatest pleasures—
paying the last installment.
                        —Paul Harwitz.

Panned Economy
Some people scatter their
    cash like rain.
That isn't true of the thrifty
    folk
Who stick to budgets and
    thus maintain
An orderly way of being
    broke.
          —Georgie Starbuck Galbraith.

Dollar Sign
Rich is when you have
trouble remembering whether
you have two or three kids
in college.
                        —Robert Fuoss.

Independent Banker
An old country gentleman
revealed to a friend that he
kept all his savings in a shoe
box under his bed. "But,
John," protested his friend,
"you should keep your
savings in the bank! Otherwise
you will lose interest."
"Oh no," came the reply,
"I always tuck a little extra in
the mattress to take care of
the interest."
                        —Lane Olinghouse.

Inheritance Tax
"Am I mentioned in the
will?" the young nephew
asked anxiously.
"You certainly are," the
lawyer replied. "Right here in
the third paragraph your

Dollar Signs

"Money-y-y…Money-y-y…Money…"

uncle says, 'I bequeath $100,000 to my niece, Sarah; $50,000 to my cousin, Janice; and to my nephew Charles, who was always curious to know if he was mentioned in my will, I say—Hi Charles!' "
—Robert Fuoss.

I-O-Who?
The problem with the U.S.
  debt,
I'm not afraid to say it,
Is not that it's so very large
Nor that we'll fail to pay it.

The problem as it stands right
  now,
As best the nation knows it,
We're half a trillion in the
  red
And no one knows who
  owes it.
—Harry Chernoff.

To My Banker
Though your high interest
  rates
Appeal to me,
They never seem
Very real to me,
And I think I've discovered
  the flaw;
I can't wait six months to
  withdraw.
—Florence Wahl Otter.

Daffynitions
Counterfeit coin: quacksilver.
—Joyce Dillingham.

Dollar Signs

IOU: Paper wait.
      —Doris Dolphin.

Inheritance: will-gotten gains.
      —Frank Tyger.

Idle Rich: people who are
rusting on their laurels.
      —Len Elliott.

Crop Support

A gentleman farmer is a
fellow who makes more hay
in one day at the office than
he does in a season on his
six-hundred-acre spread.
      —Robert Fuoss.

Candid Comment

A problem with having lots
of money is that you have to
keep watching those who are
paid to look after it.

Over Stuffed

Padded expense accounts are
common
When one's finances must be
bolstered,
But some I've seen added,
Aren't just padded,
But completely re-upholstered.
      —Edward F. Dempsey.

Parity

["*The dollar's shrinking
value abroad isn't keeping
Americans home this
summer.*"—*WSJ news item*]
Despite the dollar's status
I still intend to roam;
It may have shrunk abroad
But it also shrank at home.
      —Arnold J. Zarett.

Raised Voice

Raising plants is plenty tough,
Raising children's hard
enough,
Raising on one's head a
bump
Takes a pretty painful thump.
But, and I'm not being funny,
Worst of all is raising money.
      —Richard Armour.

Nothing New

When the term "old money"
is referred to,
More is meant than living
wage;
But my income disappears so
quickly,
It never gets a chance to
age.
      —Rosemarie Williamson.

No Accounting for It!

Our cash receipts have really
slowed
So much, it's unbelievable!
It seems the dollars that
we're owed
Are now Accounts Deceivable.
      —David N. Lawrence.

No Telling

They say he's a man of
untold wealth,
Which reminds me that on
occasion
A person of untold wealth
may be
Someone guilty of tax
evasion.
      —Richard Armour.

Mystery

Don't you sometimes
wonder how the average
person manages to scrape up
enough just to keep on being
average?
      —Edward Stevenson.

Candid Comment

An after dinner mint is the
money we need to pay the
check in most restaurants.
      —Shelby Friedman.

Final Accounting

The way people use their
credit cards, they must have
a "debt wish."

VI POLITICS

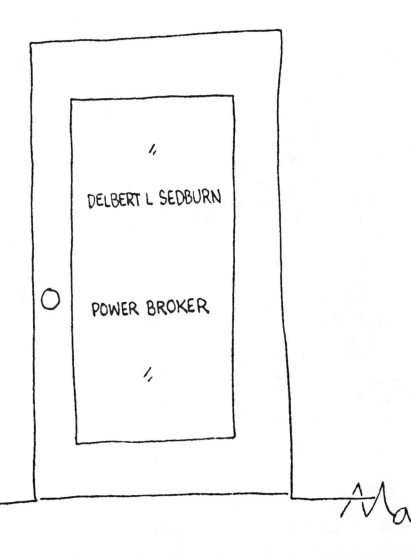

Electioneering

"The latest poll shows me with a large lead.
Sixty-eight percent of the voters mistrust
my opponent while only 51% mistrust me."

Grimm Fable

A little girl asked her mother if all fairy tales began with "Once upon a time."

"No, dear," replied Mom, "today most of them begin with, 'If I am elected.'"

Bulletin

I read a lot of papers
And it's well that I should;
Only trouble is the news
Is too true to be good.

—Herm Albright.

Clouded Forecast

His schemes sound great in
   theory,
But in practice tend to fizzle;
His concept of a brainstorm
Is often just a drizzle.

—Rosemarie Williamson.

Matter of Opinion

Opinion polls
Give me a start,
When the polls and I
Are polls apart.

—Richard Armour.

Political Prescription

A ten-term Congressman was asked how he managed always to be re-elected. "Easy," he replied. "Identify your major supporters. Then make sure that more of them are appointed than disappointed."

—Robert Fuoss.

Electioneering

Calling All Voters
Vehement critics of politics
Are rather puzzling souls.
Why do they protest in the
    street
Instead of at the polls?
                —Darrell H. Bartee.

Second Term
    Remember that fellow
who, two years ago, won a
seat in Congress on the
grounds that we need new
ideas and new faces? Well,
he's running for re-election,
only this time he advocates
keeping an experienced hand
at the tiller.
                —Robert Fuoss.

Balancing Act
As a middle of the roader,
His political future looks
    bright,
For he's holding the center
    firmly by,
Making promises left and
    right.
                —Edward F. Dempsey.

Mr. Candidate Answers the Question
"I'm glad you asked me that,
    my friend,
And in sincerity.
Let me applaud this evidence
Of your sagacity,
To start with: Simple civic
    pride

Compels me, candidly,
To reaffirm my faith in you,
Our backbone nationally.
I say again that times like
    these
Demand integrity!
Next question."
                —John C. Friedmann.

Before the Ballot
"I'll lower taxes!" This one
    shrills,
As voting day draws near;
"I'll solve all problems! That
    one claims,
"Put eggs in every beer!"

As up and down the land
    they march,
I think we're all agreed,
There's very little doubt that
    things
Look promising indeed.
                —Dick Emmons.

Sweet November
Oh, to hear one candidate
Above the general din
Declare it's barely possible
That he just might not win!
                —Bert Kruse.

Presumption
    He who promises there'll
be jobs for all has the
ridiculous idea that everybody
wants to work.
                —Ted R. Ashby.

In the Saddle
    [*"Nomination is
tantamount to election."—
News Item*]
Behold the mighty
    tantamount,
Well-known in every section.
The nominee climbs on his
    back
And rides him to election.

The nomination is the step
That counts, he is aware,
But once he mounts the
    tantamount
He's just as good as there.
                —Richard Armour.

Matter of Expediency
    Some candidates seem to
throw their hats into the ring
when their heads get too big
for them.
                —H. E. Martz.

Selective Electing
Some people study the polls
And carefully take note,
But I am one who'll never
Let one influence my vote.

In the democratic process
I am a strong believer,
So—eeny, meeny, miny, mo,
Before I pull the lever.
                —Arnold J. Zarett.

Electioneering

Voter Emoters
The biggest complainers
(I note with malice)
Are those who didn't
Cast their ballots
— Robert Gordon.

Sober Reflection
I believe in the two party system—but not in the same night.
— Lucille S. Harper.

Puzzle
Ever since election, we've been trying to figure out where some people's voter apathy leaves off and their year-round everyday indifference begins.
— Edward Stevenson.

Voters' View
The prospects
Are dismal
For those not
Charismal.
— E. B. de Vito.

Candid Comment
Mincing your words makes it easier if you later have to eat them.
— Franklin P. Jones.

Skeleton Key
One of the best ways to get a detailed genealogical picture of your family tree is to run for office.
— Robert Fuoss.

Cheers, Not Tears
Look on the bright side of
the political scene,
Despite the fact that you're
dejected—
For no matter how things
may go,
Only one of them can be
elected.
— R. M. Walsh.

Biographical Note
The candidate never wore
diapers
As a baby, 'way back when;
It seems that no one could
ever
Pin him down, even then.
— George O. Ludcke.

Daffynitions
Repartee: Remarksmanship.
— Frank Tyger.

Political platform: preach of promise.
— Arnold Glasow.

The Timing of the Shrewd
As election campaigns begin
to heat up,
Candidates are out kissing
babies
And answering questions on
issues
With firm, unequivocal
"maybes."
They're busy explaining their
own pet schemes
To save the nation from
schisms,
And greeting each voter with
handshakes
And friendly "Where-are-
euphemisms."
They know, if elected, that
they can blame
All problems on their
predecessors;
And, if they're defeated, they
all become
Infallible second-guessers.
— George O. Ludcke.

Pollster Gist
Asked if he planned to vote for a certain Congressman, the commuter said, "Well, maybe, but he's my second choice."
"Who's your first choice?" the questioner insisted.
"Almost anybody," came the reply.
— Lane Olinghouse.

Throwaways
Around election time
I always grow bitter—
Not about issues,
Just about litter.
— Arnold J. Zarett.

Electioneering

Crop Shot

If this turns out to be a traditional election year, we'll probably see the American farm problem solved once again.

    —Franklin P. Jones.

Pot Shot

To the GOP the elephant
Is the animal that is relevant;
The donkey suits the
    Democratic view.
But, getting down to the
    nitty-gritty,
It's the feeding of the kitty
That's most vital in the
    politicking zoo!

    —G. O. Ludcke.

Protective Posture

Many a politician "stands on his record" to prevent its being examined.

    —Gertrude Olinghouse.

A Political?

When delegates meet
You just know each seat
Is a base of good intentions.
But I'd like to know
Where the platforms go
At the close of the
    conventions.

    —John P. Broderick.

Candidate Distillate

For his campaign promises,
His memory goes lame;
And yet this self-same
    memory
Recalls us each by name.

    —Bill Gillick.

Social Note

Conventions are something most people leave behind when they attend one.

    —Gertrude Olinghouse.

Election Reflection

[*"—observers see a decline in American political humor . . ."—WSJ editorial*]
Though the late campaign
    had no humorous vein,
Laughter's future is not so
    precarious;
You must admit that some of
    it—
In retrospect—was hilarious.

    —E. V. Girand.

Poll Cad

He used to greet me on the
    street,
The candidate I selected,
And how his honest eyes
    would shine
When he made himself, for
    me and mine
Available at any time—
Until he was elected.

    —E. B. de Vito.

Instant Poll-itics

When great-grandfather cast
    his vote
Things took more time to be
    done—
And often a month went by
    before
It was known which man had
    won.

Later, when grandpa went to
    the polls,
In one week the newspapers
    stated
(With reasonable certainty)
Who'd be inaugurated.

In father's era the radio
    came,
And then the voting machine,
So a waiting nation knew the
    next day
Results on the political scene.

Today there are modern
    research polls
Which, by scientific detection,
Predict the winner on TV
    screens
The night before the election.

Such technology is impressive,
But I'd like to have it noted
That I don't like to be
    counted out—
Before I've even voted!

    —G.O. Ludcke.

Politicking Process

"Then shall I put you down as violently opposed?"

Mixed Meanings

Good representation: When a Congressman gets federal funds for his district.

Boondoggling: When it's not our district.

—Frank Rose.

Cynic Route

You're an old-timer if you remember a time when politicians could buy a whole ward for what a few seconds on TV cost today.

—Arnold H. Glasow.

Prelude

I raise both eyebrows
When these words I hear:
"I welcome the investigation,
I have nothing to fear."
They usually come the week
preceding
The reconsidered guilty
pleading.

—Dow Richardson.

Gun Ho!

["Sales of toy guns are expected to fall off sharply this year because of movements against war and violence."—News item.]
Toy guns, it seems, aren't
selling well,
The plastic, not the steel
ones.
I don't recall, though, having
heard

Politicking Process

In recent months, a single
word
Of lessened sales of real
ones.
—Richard Armour.

Mitigating Circumstances
In sentencing a convicted
politician to a minimum jail
term, the judge said he was
giving favorable consideration
to the fact that the defendant
did not plan to write a novel.
—Edward Stevenson.

For the Record
Lobbyists: People who go
to Washington to mix
business with pressure.
—Lane Olinghouse.

Overworked
Of course the truth hurts.
You would, too, if you were
stretched so much.
—Franklin P. Jones.

Well-Heeled
Time was when "A man of
stature"
Meant his character was
highly rated;
The reason today may simply
be
That his heels are elevated.
—George O. Ludcke.

Political Promise
It's okay if candidates
elected this fall claim to have
received a mandate from the
people. Let's just stipulate that
it is a mandate—and not a
credit card!
—Robert Fuoss.

Daffynition
Congressional jaunt:
legalized gamboling.
—Frank Tyger.

Sign Language
Posted in a California
public high school: "In the
Event of an Earthquake, the
Supreme Court Ruling Against
Prayer in School Will Be
Temporarily Suspended."
—Paul Harwitz.

Observation Point
Asked to describe the
Capitol building, a sight-seer
replied, "Outside marble.
Inside garble."

New Breed
For years the guinea pig
reproduced faster than any
other creature on earth. Then
along came the government
bureaucrat.
—Lane Olinghouse.

Stopping the Buck
Rather than more fact-
finding committees, we need
a few fact-facing committees
in Congress.
—Lane Olinghouse.

Short Sheets
The reason politicians
make strange bedfellows is
because they all use the same
bunk!
—Paul Harwitz.

Daffynitions
Non-aggression Pacts:
prints of peace.

Statesman: A man who
plays both ends against the
muddle.
—Raymond J. Cvikota.

Propaganda: Artificial
dissemination.
—H. E. Martz.

Nepotism: all the kin's
men.
—Honey Greer.

Picket Line
It would be much easier
to love the Government if the
people who went on strike
were those collecting your
taxes instead of those
collecting your garbage.
—Robert Fuoss.

Politicking Process

In-Words, Potomac Style
If on "consensus" you are
    bankin'
For an in-word, you're in a
    fix.
Much better is, "Let's first
    crank in
The intangibles." Or, "Vary
    the mix."
          —T. J. Kallsen.

Federalinguistics
Now that "to finalize" in
    Washington is out
And "to under-utilize" is just
    about—
May "excess capability," like
    them both,
Acquire the status of
    malignant growth.
          —T. J. Kallsen.

Holiday Afterthought
    What the world needs is
more mistletoe and less
missile talk.
          —Anna Herbert.

View From the Middle
Politics, it seems to me,
For years, or all too long,
Has been concerned with
    right and left
Instead of right and wrong.
          —Richard Armour.

Sample of One
I waited for years for the
    pollsters to seek

My opinion on matters of
    state:
On ecology or the SST
Or busing to integrate.
My big moment came in the
    mail today
With questionnaire provided.
So what did I do to state my
    view?
I said I was undecided.
          —Robert Fuoss.

Rueful Reflection
    The way our world is
going these days, it seems
that map makers are the only
people who can draw folks
closer together.
          —Arnold H. Glasow.

Daffynitions
    Latin American politics:
ruler derby.
          —Frank Tyger.

    Diplomacy: the art of
solving a world crisis by
creating a new one.
          —Harold Coffin.

All in the Family?
Some folks always run to
    Washington
With one problem or another,
And, once there, the Great
    White Father
Turns them over to Big
    Brother.
          —G. O. Ludcke.

Permanent Solution
We've permanent press
And permanent crease,
But we've no success
With permanent peace.

Which means, I suppose,
That we ought to ask
The makers of clothes
To take over the task,

While statesmen who balance
Land, sea, and air
Would turn their talents
To ready-to-wear.
          —Richard Armour.

Self Service
Getting federal funds for your
    group,
While preaching self-reliance,
Has now surpassed an art
    form
And become a political
    science.
          —Edward F. Dempsey.

Soft Sell
It is said that the true
    diplomat
Is one with that rare verbal
    knack
Of saying, "Go to hell" so
    attractively—
You can hardly wait to pack!
          —G. O. Ludcke.

Tranquil Times
    ["*People are complacent,
they don't seem to care.*

Politicking Process

*They're apathetic and
resigned."—News Item.*]
Where once the natives
Rose in wrath,
Where once were wroth
Or zestful,
Today they take another path;
The natives are getting
Restful.
　　　　　—Dow Richardson.

Daffynitions
Frankincense: public
reaction to congressional
mailing privileges.
　　　　　—Grant Stockdale.

Missile launch site: soar
spot.
　　　　　—Shelby Friedman.

Literary Lapse
If truth in labeling is the law,
Someone's guilty of
　　dereliction—
When certain political memoirs
Can be listed under non-
　　fiction.
　　　　　—Edward F. Dempsey.

No Mistaking Identity
Printed on a card found
in a Congressman's wallet: "In
case of accident, call a press
conference."

Legislative Mode
Congress opens with a
prayer and closes with a
probe.
　　　　　—Arnold Glasow.

Good Question
If we meant to give away
the Canal, why did we install
locks on it?
　　　　　—Steven F. Shulman.

Issues And Answers
When a politician changes
his position it's sometimes
hard to tell whether he has
seen the light or felt the
heat.
　　　　　—Robert Fuoss.

Slow Grind
Certain procedures and
　　processes
Are enough to give one
　　pause;
Two things we should never
　　observe being made
Are sausages—and laws.
　　　　　—George Ludcke.

A Word to the Wise
That Presidents do not do
　　better,
Despite their many capers,
Surprises me since they
　　receive
Advice from all newspapers.
　　　　　—Gloria H. Cole.

Diplomatic Language
Countries that want to be
recognized seldom want to be
recognized for what they are.
　　　　　—Robert Fuoss.

Fitting Punishment
Don't send to jail
Or fix high bail
For politicians who are
　　crooks.
But give just desserts
Right where it hurts
By banning all their books.
　　　　　—Leonard Dittell.

Fare Enough?
Congressional junkets
Are costly and wrong.
I wish they would stop them,
Or take me along.
　　　　　—Richard Armour.

Quick Change
Our esteem for politicians
Today is so fickle that,
Sometimes they're barely
　　sworn in
Before they're being sworn at.
　　　　　—Edward F. Dempsey.

Open Season
Our life, liberty and pursuit of
　　happiness
Are fairly safe from
　　oppression;
Except for during those

Politicking Process

months of the year
When legislatures are in
  session.
                —George O. Ludcke.

The Limit
[*"Violations of 200-mile
fishing limit have international
implications"—News Note.*]
How to deal with foreign
  violators
Is becoming increasingly
  delicate;
Surely they can't be sticking
Their nets out just for the
  halibut!
                —George O. Ludcke.

Men From Mars
Life on planets other than
earth seems very unlikely.
Despite numerous deep space
probes there have been no
new applicants for foreign aid.
                —Robert Fuoss.

Daffynitions
United Nations building:
World Tirade Center.
                —Frank Tyger.

Exile: foreign languish.
                —Leon Elliott.

Idi Amin: African violent.
                —Bruce B. Randall Jr.

Political Paradox
Last year, our
Congressman was campaigning
as the man with the answers.
So now, why is he sending
us so many questionnaires?
                —Arch Napier.

Science Note
If Red China launches a
spy in the sky satellite, it can
be called a Peking Tom.
                —Shelby Friedman.

Hidden Liabilities
It's quickly becoming an
  axiom
Or at least a pretty good bet
That the richer a politician is
The more likely he's deep in
  debt.
                —R. C. Shelbelski.

Limb-o
All we used to have were
foot races. Now we have
arms races.
                —Maurice Seitter.

Raunchy Launching
What's wrong with the
railroads? Well, if you look at
their stations you realize
they're suffering from a
terminal illness.
                —Robert Fuoss.

Candid Comment
It's the opinion of some
that crops could be grown on
the moon. Which raises a
fear that it may not be long
before we're paying somebody
not to.
                —Franklin P. Jones.

Daffynitions
Space probe: pry in the
sky.
                —Honey Greer.

Gun control: trigger mortis.
                —LeRoy London.

Pacifist: flag-waiver.
                —Doris Dolphin.

Pollution and the Environment

"Gee! The seventy-sixth floor! Right up where the photochemical particulants meet the clouds!"

Pollution Confusion
This matter of environment
Is as confusing as can be.
I wonder, am I harming it
As much as it is harming
me?
—Erma Lea Chitty.

Earthly Advice
When prosecuting polluters, let the punishment fit the grime.
—Frank Tyger.

Name Drip
Some people who can discuss ecology pretentiously didn't even know there was such a word a few years ago.
—Paul Tulien.

Slips at Sea
One more oil spill from a
tanker
Should cause the U.S.A. a lot
of rancor.
In spite of America's lenience
We should disallow those
Flags of Convenience.
—Peter Lind Hayes.

Bulletin Board
The new wave of young conservationists are known as Thoreau-breds.
—Raymond J. Cvikota.

Pollution and the Environment

Slick System
If all this spilling of oil at
    sea,
By tankers, doesn't stop
We can quit drilling under
    the ocean floor
And just skim it off the top.
          —George O. Ludcke.

Ecology Note
    It used to be that folks
hoped to see America first.
Now we're hoping to see it
last!
          —Arnold Glasow.

Signs of Progress
They're cutting down the
    trees
And chopping at the bramble
In all those nearby woods
Through which I used to
    ramble.
A tractor and a pile of mud
Block where I used to enter.
And what'll rise in place of
    this?
Why, another shopping center.
          —Robert Gordon.

Dry Gulched
We're implored to conserve
    precious water—
And we do, for "conditions
    are dire."
Then we're told that due to
    this lost revenue
Water bills must be hiked that
    much higher!
          —Bert Murray.

Bang-Up Thought
    Every time I see a picture
of the surface of the moon I
wonder if maybe their
scientists came up with the
bomb a few years before ours
did.
          —Robert Fuoss.

Handle With Care
    ["*A one-degree variation
in the position of the earth's
axis would cause untold
human suffering.*"—*Editorial
note.*]
On very critical tolerances
The universe is built;
We hope there's a celestial
    sign out there
That reads very plainly,
    "Don't tilt!"
          —George O. Ludcke.

Rough Sailing
Water pollution is getting so
    bad
It's really making me jumpy!
In our area, for instance,
Even our water beds are
    lumpy.
          —Ruth M. Walsh.

Daffynitions
    Forest pollution: a vice in
the wilderness.
          —Raymond J. Cvikota.

    Soil erosion: terrain
robbery.
          —Arnold H. Glasow.

Air pollution: domain
poisoning.

    Litterbug: strewball.
          —Honey Greer.

    Defiled landscape:
Obscenery.
          —H. E. Martz.

Hidden Wonder
    "We've heard so much
about your famous smog," the
visitor to Southern California
told her host, "we certainly
hope the weather clears up
enough for us to see it."
          —Edward Stevenson.

Root Problem
    The water shortage is so
bad, if you live in the West,
you don't talk to your plants
—you apologize to them.
          —Bob Orben.

Pollution Blues
The air we breathe is
    poisoned,
Our rivers are filled with
    guck,
You've got to watch the
    beaches
Or you'll drown in the oily
    muck.

The fish are gasping in the
    depths
As they struggle to and fro,
While ships above flush out

Pollution and the Environment

their wastes
On the choking life below.

Our roads are trails of empty
cans,
And litter by the ton,
And all along the broken
glass
Glistens in the sun.

We still can sing of beauty,
In this land of the proud and
free,
But wealth and waste have
changed us
To the "Effluent Society."
—Ron Moxness.

Environmental Echo
There must be better ways
to keep America green than
to have the whole country in
a pickle.
—Robert Orben.

Original Earth Woman
Great-grandma practiced
ecology by making use of
things we throw away today.
Only to her it was economy.
—Paul Tulien.

Nature Lover
When asked why he had
moved out of the Los
Angeles area, the actor
replied, "I got tired of waking
up every morning to the
sound of birds coughing."
—C. McClure.

Grime Doesn't Pay?
Our detergents, it seems, are
polluting the streams;
Paper towels add to waste,
we're aware;
And the coal we devour for
that hot, soothing shower
Sends its smoke and smut
into the air.

I can't help but conclude, as
I wistfully brood
On a future that looks none
too purty,
That our planet would be a
lot cleaner, you see,
If we'd all do our part, and
stay dirty.
—G. Sterling Leiby.

Prayer
Now I lay me down to sleep,
I pray, somehow, my soul to
keep
From noxious fumes which
autos throw,
And color television's glow;
From water swallowed at the
beach,
And ear-destroying sonic
screech;
From nicotine and mercury,
And that old devil, DDT.
And last, I pray this prayer
defends
Me from pollution-minded
friends.
—Betty Billipp.

Polluters' Progress
Anti-litter campaigns do
have their effect. More and
more people now look
around to see if anybody's
watching before they throw
down a wrapper.
—Lane Olinghouse.

Population Problems

"As if the illegal alien problem isn't bad enough already!"

No Growth Vote
Show me a little town that's
    sort of backward,
Not concerned about its
    "image" or its size,
Where the people do not call
    themselves "dynamic"
And there's no tremendous
    drive to modernize;
Where they're not perpetually
    promoting "progress"
And never really had the
    urge to boost—
And I'll show you a place
    that's going nowhere,
But undoubtedly a lovely
    place to roost.
          —Sam Hudson.

Up Tight
This is the space age
Yet I feel gloom—
Wherever I go
There is no room.
          —Arnold J. Zarett.

Development
Where once the tended
    orchard grew
And whitely bloomed the
    plum,
Stands now a quite expensive
    new
Condominium.

From it no branch, flower-
    laden, grows;
In it there sings no linnet;
I should be grateful, I
    suppose—
Since I am living in it.
          —Rachel Mack.

Population Problems

Mixed Meanings
Over-population: how we think of a neighbor's large family.

Blessed event: an addition to ours.
— Frank Rose.

Canape
If the population explosion continues, the world will be like one big cocktail party: Too many people and not enough food.
— Tom Fallon.

Southern Exposure
[*"Suddenly just about everyone has rediscovered the nation's sunny southland."*— *WSJ editorial.*]
With the growth of population
In the southern states being
    felt,
Uncle Sam may have to let
    out a few
More notches in his Sun Belt.
— George O. Ludcke.

Vox Pop
The population slowdown
    shows
We're mending all our fences;
We've taken lots of good
    advice
And coming to our census
— E. B. de Vito.

Flying Sorcerers
[*"The FAA says the nation's commuter airlines will be carrying 15 million passengers annually by 1989. . . ." WSJ item*]
The Brothers Wright deserve
    applause,
And bravos, cheers and raves
    because
Their bright idea of aviation
Has solved our over-
    population;
By keeping millions in the air
We're thinning out the crowds
    down here!
— Gloria Rosenthal.

Legalities

Time Out!
During the questioning of prospective jurors, one citizen exclaimed, "I'm sorry, Judge! I can't serve on the jury. One look at that man and I'm convinced he's guilty!"

"You are looking," said the Judge, "at the district attorney."
— D. B. Brown.

The Old Know-How
"No-fault insurance hasn't affected my practice adversely," said the lawyer. "After all, it still takes us pros to figure out whose no-fault it is."
— Edward Stevenson.

Daffynitions
Detective's file: Clues closet.
— Arthur P. Grossman.

Police expenditures: fuzz budget.
— Frank Tyger.

Hereinafter: where lawyers go when they die.
— Paul Harwitz.

Prison riots: stir wars.
— Daisy Brown.

Legalities

"Since we've been using recycled paper, I don't feel too guilty about all this."

Cash award in a slander suit: Slur tax.
> —Edward Stevenson.

Jail: Repenthouse.
> —Jack Kraus.

Death Trap
"Do you believe in capital punishment?" the district attorney asked the prospective juror.
"Yes, sir, I do," replied the latter, "just so long as it is not too severe."
> —Lane Olinghouse.

Warning
[*"Epidemic of Arson"*— *News Story Headline.*]
Apparently, some businessmen
(Of course, we'll use no names)
Have found that profits going down
Can still go up: in flames.
> —Fred S. Buschmeyer Jr.

By Any Other Name
"Stone walls do not a prison make"
In this semantic age;
They make a "correctional facility"
That's nonetheless a cage!
> —Dal Devening.

Legalities

Character Study
Most process servers have a lien and hungry look.
— Robert Fuoss.

Word Play
The reason crime doesn't pay is that when it does they call it something else.
— Franklin P. Jones.

Pure-ocracy
It's anybody's guess—why we have over thirty million laws trying to enforce the Ten Commandments.
— Abbe Rich.

Trial and Terror
Each man's allowed his day
   in court,
Due process is his right, in
   short,
But with the various delays,
Motions, challenges, and stays,
It seems, before the trial's
   through,
That there's much undue
   process, too.
— Donna Evleth.

Telling It Like It Was
When the jury failed to reach a verdict in a cut-and-dried case, the judge said disgustedly, "I discharge this jury!" At which point, an irate member called out, "You can't do that!"

"Did I understand you correctly? You have received a summons for jaywalking and you wish to plea bargain?"

Legalities

"And why not?" asked the judge.

"Because you didn't hire me," said the juror, pointing to the lawyer for the defense. "He did!"

—Thomas Henry.

Social Comment

Nowadays, criminals know their rights better than their wrongs.

—Arnold Glasow.

Worth a Try

"It's bad enough when shoplifters steal you blind," the storekeeper complained to one of his clerks, "but when they try to return the merchandise for credit because they don't think it's up to snuff, that's too much!"

"Do you think it would help, Boss," the clerk suggested hopefully, "if we put up a sign saying 'All Thefts Final?'"

—Edward Stevenson.

Court Order

Foreign observers are sometimes bewildered by America's criminal justice system. Why, they ask, do you lock up the jury and turn the accused loose on bail?

—Robert Fuoss.

Daffynitions

Subpoena: bringing home the beckon.

—Raymond J. Cvikota.

Policemen's Strike: copout.

Bulletproof vests: deflective merchandise.

—Frank Tyger.

Legal Battle: brief encounter.

—Fletcher D. Slater.

Police Department shake-ups: cop rotation,

—Mary Lee Sauermann.

Alibi: Slip cover.

—Selma Glasser.

Repentence

The judge appraised the prisoner sternly and said, "You were caught stealing from a silo. What do you have to say for yourself?"

"I realize now," replied the culprit meekly, "that they were ill-gotten grains."

—Shelby Friedman.

Citizen's Complaint

To do my civic duty as a
    juror I did try,
But it nearly drove me crazy.
    Please let me tell you why.

The judge and the two
    lawyers seemed to thrive
    upon delays;
It seemed "recess," "adjourn,"
    "retire" was all I heard for
    days.
And when at length the jury
    reached a verdict, in
    rapport—
They called us back and told
    us they had settled out of
    court.

—Louise J. Panni.

Energy

Sunspot
   One good thing about
solar-energy is that you can
look up and see how much
is left.
> —Paul Harwitz.

Temperature Tantrums
Some argue it won't work,
Others say it can't be beat;
That's how solar energy,
So far, generates heat.
> —Arnold J. Zarett.

Easy Does It
My winter energy saving plan
Needed no congressional
   approval,
For after each storm
I'd wait till it's warm—
And use solar-powered snow
   removal.
> —Edward F. Dempsey.

Wet Strength
   [*"Energy shortage prompts
renewal of proposals to
harness ocean power."—News
note.*]
The importance of finding
   new energy
Cannot be denied—
But the sea doesn't always
   cooperate;
Sometimes it's not fit to be
   tide.
> —George O. Ludcke.

"Power corrupts and a power shortage
corrupts absolutely."

Energy

Overt Action

A certain fellow plans to register as a foreign agent. If his fuel bills keep going up, he expects to spend most of the coming winter working for the OPEC nations.

—Edward Stevenson.

Process of Elimination

It's feared by many that world resources are dwindling at a rate so rapid that soon there will be nothing left for nations to fight over.

—Lane Olinghouse.

No Solution

Instead of oil calming troubled waters, it now makes waters troubled.

—H. E. Martz.

VII CONSUMER CONSUMED

"Until this moment, I never realized we needed a
food chopper with a built-in transistor radio."

Emptor's Caveats

"It's true—gravely flakes *do* make clothes blacker than black."

Revised Edition
"Let the buyer beware," the
    phrase once read,
For many an ancient plier.
But as shoplifting climbs,
It could read in our times
"Let the seller beware of the
    buyer."
          —Edward F. Dempsey.

Supermarket Blues
There's a futile feeling of
    helpless distress
When you're in the line
    marked
"Six Items or Less"
And the aggressive lady in
    front of you
Has twenty-two.
         —Colleen Stanley Bare.

Q and A
    Veteran researchers report
increasing difficulty in
completing national surveys. It
seems we now have so many
polls there's a shortage of
opinions to fill them.
         —Robert Fuoss.

Safe and Sound
We have a safe deposit box
Which hasn't much inside.
But getting to it, with our key
And proof of our identity,
Gives us a certain pride.
         —Richard Armour.

Emptor's Caveats

Cluckster

If you produce some useful
    things,
You doubtless want to sell
    them,
But folks won't come to you
    unless
Persistently you tell them.

The hen has known this
    secret long,
For there's no creature wiser,
She cackles when she's laid
    her egg,
The world's first advertiser!
        —Paul Tulien.

Present Tins

[*"More than six-hundred
sizes, shapes and styles of tin
cans are manufactured by
American can firms today."—
News item*]
I've always known there were
    a lot
Of shapes and styles of cans,
    but not
Six-hundred quite. However,
    now
I think of it, I have to bow
To this statistic. Every mode
I think I've seen beside the
    road.
        —Richard Armour.

Mixed Meanings

Shopping: When customers
ask to see something more
expensive.
Buying: When they ask to
see something cheaper.

Free Press

I hang around
Until I've scanned
Each magazine
Upon the stand,
Taking care
The while I eye them
Not to tear nor soil—
Nor buy them.
        —Sheldon White.

Store Card

"Do you realize that for
each of the past thirty-two
weeks you've been advertising
a new 'Greatest Sale Ever'?"
said the man from the Better
Business Bureau to the owner
of the discount store.

"Yes," the owner admitted
ruefully. "Sometimes even I
wonder how we do it!"

The Catch

Those fifty-percent-off sales
have only one thing wrong
with them. The price the fifty
percent comes off is usually
one-hundred percent too high.
        —Edward Stevenson.

Cents-Off Relief

Remember when a
coupon-clipper was a
bondholder in a bank? Now
it's a housewife in a
supermarket.
        —Arch Napier.

Fuel for Thought

America: where you can
see people who make
$25,000 a year pump their
own gas—while a kid gets
paid $3.60 an hour to sit on
a stool and watch them.
        —Bob Orben.

Buy-Buy Blues

Of all the sighs
I sigh for naught,
My saddest sigh:
"I could have bought—"
        —Bob Herz.

Sign Language

On the window of a
novelty shop: "We have a
complete line of all the things
you can do without."
        —Pru Pratt.

Dead Line

A businessman handed
the hotel manager a bouquet
of flowers and said
sympathetically, "It's for your
switchboard operator."

The manager said with a
smile, "Thank you, sir. I'm
sure she will appreciate your
compliment to her fine
service."

"Service!" moaned the
businessman. "I was under
the impression she had
passed away!"

Emptor's Caveats

Hard Bargain
Trading stamps give lots of
    pleasure,
And they promise us great
    treasure;
Silver, clocks, refrigerators,
Handbags made of alligators.
But I guess I'm sorta funny—
Couldn't I just have the
    money?
    —R. V. McIntyre.

Upper Cuss
Much to the delight of
the restaurant's waiters, the
manager posted a sign
reading, "Customers who
think our waiters are rude
should see the manager."

Ad Glib
Five words which never
Make me scurry:
"Supply is limited,
So hurry!"
    —Stephen Schlitzer.

Sticky
"This glue is guaranteed,"
the salesgirl declared. "Even if
it doesn't hold anything
together, you'll be stuck with
it."

And Face the Music!
When you buy things for
a song, watch out for the
accompaniment.
    —F. G. Kernan.

Daffynitions
Introductory offer: padded
sell.
    —Robert Fuoss.

Confidence man: dupe
peddler.
    —Raymond J. Cvikota.

Sales promotion: the shill
factor.
    —Robert Fuoss.

Installment Buying:
Confound interest.
    —Jack Kraus.

Bargain basement: a
cellar's market.
    —Raymond J. Cvikota.

Outdoor auctions: flea
bargaining

Telephone bill: Gab fare.
    —Honey Greer.

Information Pause
Scientists are men who
prolong life so that we can
have time to make all the
installments on the wonderful
things they invent.
    —Rose Cohen.

Libelous Label
The American public was
in trouble from the minute
manufacturers stopped calling
us customers and started
calling us consumers.
    —Robert Orben.

The Fur Hundred?
"I want to buy a dog I
can be proud of," said the
snobbish buyer. "Does this
one have a good pedigree?"
"Listen," replied the owner
of the kennel, "his pedigree is
so good that if he could talk,
he wouldn't speak to either
one of us!"
    —Paul Harwitz.

Logical Choice
An explorer returned
home from South America
with a trunkful of shrunken
heads he hoped to sell as
novelties. He phoned a local
department store and asked
to speak to someone.
"Just a moment," a voice
replied brightly. "I'll refer you
to the office of our head
buyer."
    —Lane Olinghouse.

Contrite Correspondent
My letters always open
    "Dear"
And they close "Sincerely."

Emptor's Caveats

"Now this one destroys all the dolls while
leaving the doll houses standing!"

The first shows me
    affectionate,
The second honest, clearly.

I know all this is just a form
And not believed a bit,
Yet there are times when I
    confess
I feel a hypocrite.
                    —Richard Armour.

Sign Language
    Displayed in an
optometrist's window: "If You
Don't See What You Want,
You've Come to the Right
Place."
                    —Dan Janson.

Gripevine
    "You pay a small
deposit," said the salesman,
"then you make no more
payments for six months."
    "Who told you about us?"
The customer snapped back.
                    —Paul Harwitz.

Ownership Onus
    This is still the land of
opportunity. Where else can
we get together the down
payment on so many things
we can't afford—and don't
need?
                    —Franklin P. Jones.

Emptor's Caveats

Shop Talk

Illustrating the sweet smell
of success are perfumers—
who stick their business into
other people's noses.

—Honey Greer.

Those Catalog Order Forms!

"First crease both sides,
Then fold up end;
Your order, thus,
You'll safely send.

"No staples, please,
Or sticky tape;
Your check inside
Will not escape.

"Just moisten flap—
It's gummed, that's why."
(It came unglued—
And so did I!)

—Rosemarie Williamson.

Suspicious Customer

When merchants put their
goods on sale,
How come I wear a frown?
Because I think they marked
it up
Before they marked it down.

—Dick Emmons.

Out of the Woods

[*"Many Discover Log
Houses As a Lower Cost
Way of Owning a home.
. . ."—WSJ headline.*]
As construction know-how
increases

We may reach a new
millennium:
Economical luxury living
In a log cabin condominium.

—Arnold J. Zarett.

Daffynitions

Jewelry shop: gemnasium.

—Walter Anthony.

Plastic formula: vinyl
analysis.

—Robert Fitch.

Auction sale: A lot of
sound and fury, signifying
nodding.

—Shelby Friedman.

Game show studio: guess
chamber.

—Daisy Brown.

Disposable bottle: pint of
no return.

—Robert Fitch.

Window shopper: buy
passer.

—Maurice Seitter.

Shopping center graffiti:
handwriting on the mall.

—Shelby Friedman.

Last Resort

I fit slot A inside slot B;
I jam in C and D then,
I ponder unassembled parts
And where they ought to be
then.
I jam the corners into
grooves
And hope for right selections.
Then if all else fails, of
course
I study the directions.

—Jean Conder Soule.

Scare Tactic

A collection firm, tired of
delays from debtors, came up
with a two-page letter: On
opening the envelope, the
recipient finds the first page
of the letter is missing. At the
top of the second page is
written: "Now, you wouldn't
want us to do THAT, would
you?"

—Herm Albright.

150

Not-so-lively Arts: TV, Movies, Books

NORTH GALLERY

THE ALPHEUS T. EADS IMPRINTED T-SHIRT COLLECTION →

Traditionalist

An elderly lady was looking at an art exhibition and one modern painting brought her to a dead stop.

"What in the world is that supposed to be?" she asked the artist who stood nearby.

"My dear lady," she was loftily told, "that is supposed to be a mother with her child."

"Well," snapped the old lady, "why isn't it?"

Picture Puzzle

I can't tell what those new
   painters are saying,
Although to some they're the
   new sensation,
As on canvas they keep
   throwing or spraying
The pigment of their
   imagination.
         —Leonard Dittell.

Bright Side

One reassuring thing about modern art is that things can't possibly be as bad as they are painted.

Daffynitions

Tragic opera: disaster aria.
         —Jane Hunt Clark.

Fresco: A dyed-in-the-wall painting.
         —Raymond J. Cvikota.

Not-so-lively Arts: TV, Movies, Books

Trick photography: focus-pocus.
—Doris Dolphin.

Sour notes: efface the music.

Barbershop quartet: voice squad.
—John Dratwa.

Playwright summoned for emergency re-writes: lemon aide.
—Walter Marvin.

Three-line poem: Couplet that runneth over.
—Mary Lee Sauermann.

From the Mouths of Babes
A small boy wandered into an art gallery and regarded with awe the abstract painting. "What's that?" he asked a guard.
"That's a man," the guard responded.
"And what's that?" the boy asked.
"That's his wife."
"Gee," muttered the youngster, "I certainly hope they don't have any kids!"
—Harold Helfer.

Aria Code
To sing with grand opera
Takes diaphragm power,
But to sing with abandon
Takes only a shower!
—Joyce Kirsher Megginson.

Interested Observer
A small boy was taken to a concert by his culture-conscious mother. While the soprano was at the peak of her solo, the child nudged his mother and pointed to the orchestra conductor. "Mommy," he asked, "why is that man shaking his stick at the lady?"
"He isn't dear. He's merely leading the orchestra."
"But," whispered the child, "she's the only one who's hollering!"

Catching On
We're beginning to understand the TV sportscaster. For example, when one of his favorite teams loses, that's an upset.
—Edward Stevenson.

Prime Time's Naked Truth
The TV ladies long have
    dressed
To show a length of cloven
    chest.
Now, trending down the self-
    same route,
Men dress to show the chest
    hirsute.
We viewers can't escape the
    feeling
What's going on is most
    revealing:
No cover-ups, soon; full
    disclosure—
Until there is complete
    exposure.
Flesh-barers, better have a
    care:
How much bare flesh can
    viewers bear?
—A. S. Flaumenhaft.

Daffynitions
Canned laughter: Jest desserts.
—Daisy Brown.

TV commercials: yak in the box.
—Shelby Friedman.

TV medical drama: Of Human Bandage.
—Herm Albright.

TV censor: bleeping Tom.
—Rena Greer.

Channel Chuckle
Some people think that what we have to do is get violence off the streets and back on TV where it belongs!
—Daisy Brown.

Not-so-lively Arts: TV, Movies, Books

"If you're looking for violence and excitement,
how about bathing the dog?"

Mealtime Magic
On some occasions, the most effective way to improve the flavor of a TV dinner is to turn off the TV.
—Robert Orben.

Brake-Off
They call those pauses station breaks,
But I ask, for my information,
Why six commercials is what it takes
To identify the station?
—S. S. Biddle.

Fan Fare
The television-addicted tot answered the front doorbell and, discovering a brush salesman on the steps, called out, "Hey, Mommy, it's a live commercial!"
—Herm Albright.

T.V. Dropout
An airplane has been hijacked
And ransom is demanded.
Warfare's breaking out somewhere,
A spy has been remanded.
A government is cracking down,
A counterplot is cooking
I think if you will pardon me,
I'll simply give up looking.
—Robert Gordon.

153

Not-so-lively Arts: TV, Movies, Books

Mind Over Matter
Some people are finding television quite educational—it's driving them back to books.

—Herm Albright.

TV Talk Show-Offs
I view the glittering guests as
  pests
When what it's all about
Is that they're there
To hawk their wares
Or else to hype and tout.

—E. B. de Vito.

Sneak Preview
For those impatient masochists among its readers, a TV magazine recently offered an advance look at next season's programs.

—Edward Stevenson.

Status Quo Woe
It may be that the world isn't
  any worse than it was
When I was a young go-
  getter. . . .
I think that the violence that's
  happening today
Just reflects that news
  coverage is better.

—Ruth M. Walsh.

Funny Business
When watching TV comedies,
It always seems strange to
  me,
That the laughter invariably is
  canned,
When the writers and actors
  should be.

—Edward F. Dempsey.

Cause for Alarm
Television networks are concerned by what appears to be a diminishing audience for their programs. Some alarmists are even predicting that the country is about to be engulfed in a wave of literacy.

—Edward Stevenson.

Negative Reaction
It's very obvious that
My ideas have been dated
By my amazement at how
Motion pictures are rated.
For I can remember when,
It seems a few years ago—
They wouldn't develop film
For some movies we now
  show.

—Gail Cooke.

Opinionated
Whenever a censor is
  mentioned
My temper is sorely tried—
I'll always resent a character
  who
Thinks his conscience should
  be my guide.

—Mae Woods Bell.

Popping Off
Popcorn eaters in a movie
I don't find so very groovy.
Not that I am bothered when
Kids go out, come in again.
I don't mind the popcorn
  smell,
Which I really stand quite
  well,
Nor the sound of popcorn
  crunching,
Paper rustling, people
  munching,
Nor the floor of flotsam,
  jetsam—
It's that I, at last, must get
  some!

—Richard Armour.

Unsettling Experience
We saw a G-rated film the other night, and while it was great not to have to sit through two hours of sex or violence, it sure was scary in that big dark theater all by ourselves.

—Edward Stevenson.

Daffynitions
Angry glances: stare wars.

—Bert Murray.

Censorship Board: tsk force.

—Robert Fuoss.

Not-so-lively Arts: TV, Movies, Books

"I liked the part that we're not old enough to understand."

Starlight, Starblight

"One of the joys of being a movie columnist," the writer said, "is helping some struggling unknown actor achieve success, putting him on a pedestal for the public to adore, and then trying to knock him off it."
—Edward Stevenson.

It Never Fails

A critic is someone who's at his best when you're at your worst.
—Tony Pettito.

Kid Stuff

Parental guidance suggested
On movies, often as not,
Means take the kids along
    with you
To help explain the plot.
—Edward F. Dempsey.

Rated Out

Films rated "X" for adults are
    fitted,
With no one under eighteen
    admitted.
I now propose, for the over
    thirty,
Films rated "Y", that are
    really dirty
And a rating of "Z", movies
    steeped in sin,
The very utlimate—no one
    gets in!
—Richard Armour.

Not-so-lively Arts: TV, Movies, Books

Axe Rating
The only thing movies and TV leave to the imagination these days is the plot.
—Paul Harwitz.

Numbed Audience
When I see a modern film or
    play,
I feel that I'm morally
    blocked;
What I find so shocking
    today
Is that I'm no longer shocked.
—May Richstone.

Waiting Game
Films nowadays
Suffer two debits:
Too short on art,
Too long on credits.
—Mimi Kay.

Cassette Vignette
At the rate cassettes are
    replacing
Books in our nation's
    classrooms today,
Yesterday's bookworms may
    well turn into
Tomorrow's tapeworms, per
    se.
—R. M. Walsh.

Literature Lagger
When people mention brand-
new books,
I always feel a lack

I'll join the conversation when
It's out in paperback.
—Dick Emmons.

Bestsellers
In older novels,
The plot would unfurl
Until the end when
The boy got the girl.
In today's novels,
It seems the gauge is:
The boy gets the girl
Every three pages.
—Gail Cooke.

Library News
There was a time when "I couldn't put it down" described an exciting book. Now it may well mean a best-seller you don't dare put down for fear your teenager will pick it up.
—Robert Fuoss.

Literary Note
So many people are writing books that "tell all"—soon we'll be having a Book of the Mouth Club.
—Robert Orben.

Literary Irony
"Crime may not pay," said the literary agent to an unpublished author, "but it can put you in touch with a publisher who does."
—G. Sterling Leiby.

Daffynitions
Rare book: One that comes back after you've lent it out.
—Paul Harwitz.

Sour recollections: memorabilious.
—Shelby Friedman.

Scandinavian verse: Norsery rhyme.
—Sam Rose.

Diary: penned-up emotions.
—Honey Greer.

Tall tale: bunk account.
—June Brady.

Plot: collusion course.
—Len Elliott.

Autobiography: Boast seller.

Saying Volumes
There is that book, you
    know, "Who's Who"
That lists name after name
Of people who are there
    because
They've made a certain fame.

But what we also need, I
    think,

Not-so-lively Arts: TV, Movies, Books

To help with tongue and pen,
Is something titled, say,
  "What's What"—
Or possibly "When's When."

"Where's Where" would also
  have its use,
I doubt that you'll deny,
But puzzled, worried as we
  are,
The best would be "Why's
  Why."

      —Richard Armour.

Literary Cycle
    It won't be long now
before you begin to see ads
for books that will cost you
$29.95 before Dec. 25 and
$35 thereafter—unless, of
course, you prefer to wait for
those Giant Clearance Sales
around Easter, when
everything goes for $4.99.
      —Edward Stevenson.

Frightening Talent
He thought that, by hiring a
  ghost writer,
The prestige was sure to
  vaunt him;
But the things to which his
  name is signed
Keep coming back to haunt
  him.
      —G. O. Ludcke.

"About this '101 Tips for Consumers'
I bought—there are only 97 tips in it."

Not-so-lively Arts: TV, Movies, Books

Fashions

A Word to Authors
I'm sick of the psyche,
I'm weary of race
And sexual inversions all over
    the place.
Ere pollution produces
Earth's terminal whirl
Can't we just have one book —
Normal boy meets sane girl?
      —Vinton Liddell Pickens.

"I'll take this one."

Fashions

Sounding Off
Those tiny shops with
    youthful fashions—
I like the styles; don't mind
    the crowd;
In fact, I find it's not the
    colors,
But the music that's too loud.
      —Rosemarie Williamson.

Tie Score
The ties on my tie rack
Are cherished with care;
The fifty I own—
And the five that I wear.
      —Harry Lazarus.

Ewe Tell 'Em
Wool can face competition
From synthetics without a
    quiver;
Who's heard of virgin
    polyester
And whoever saw a sheep
    shiver?
      —George O. Ludcke.

Clothes No's
In fashion when told I must
    get up-to-date,
I negate.
If they ask me to sample a
    turtleneck sweater,
I don't think I'd better.
If they recommend beads or
    a necklace of gold,
I grow cold.
And to trying on tunics like
    Nehru or Mao,
I cry, "Nao!"
      —Robert Gordon.

Figure Fallacy
Most gals will admit they paid
A ridiculous price for a dress;
But that they bought it for an
    absurd figure
Is something they won't
    confess!
      —R. M. Walsh.

Up on Fashion
The wide heel has replaced
    the spike.
(What varied styles the ladies
    like!)
A heel's in vogue, and then
    it goes—
It keeps a woman on her
    toes.
      —G. Sterling Leiby.

Hung Up
I could have cleared my
    closet
And done it with a smile,
But by the time I got to it,
My clothes were back in style.
      —Dorothy Dalton.

Rebellion
I rebel at being told
What is new and what is old,
What is out, and what is in,
In apparel, feminine.

I look absolutely grim in
Clothes designed by anti-
    women
Men, who chuckle up a
    sleeve

At women, who, sheeplike,
    believe
Fashion's edict, judgment-
    numbing:
"If it's current, it's becoming."

I reject what they assay—
I elect to be passé.
      —Annie Komorny.

Mini Unhappy Returns
For those who question the
    masculinity
Of certain French designers,
The latest collections should
    enforce
The doubts of these
    maligners.

Those lovely lengths of naked
    leg
Are out; the word is not the
    midi,
A length unflattering to the
    girl
And to the aging biddy.

Girl-watchers of the world,
    unite!
Dispel the thought it's dutiful
To follow every fashion trend.
Please keep America beautiful!
      —Jane Mishkin.

Topless Stockings?
I agree with the gentlemen
Whom I have heard
Give opinions about women's
    dress,

Fashions

And in speaking of females
In slacks have inferred
Those who wear them should
    be bottomless.

But conversely I hasten
A point to be made
Of the man who on
    weekends cavorts
All over the place
With his bare knees displayed:
There are some men who
    shouldn't wear shorts!
— Alison Wyrley Birch.

Sour Drapes
Although I've berated the
    nude look in clothes
It is not just a case of
    decorum;
I may appear dated, but
    frankly disclose
I would look a lot worse if I
    wore 'em!
— Jane Herald.

Fashion Note
    Remark of visitor from
Russia: "One of the first
things you notice in America
is the shortage of skirts."
— Lane Olinghouse.

Mini Lesson
As an economic seer,
This I plainly see,
My rate of interest's going to
    drop,

If hemlines fall below the
    knee.
— Robert W. Leach.

No Cover-Lover
The mini-skirt is great 'cause
    it
Lets front and sides and back
    see—
But now some fool's designed
    a coat
That wrecks it all—the maxi!
— Dick Emmons.

Loose Excuse
Why have I turned
My back on pants?
So friends won't laugh
At my expanse!
— Edith Ogutsch.

Aging Process
While waiting for those silver
    streaks
With which the beauty shop
    is frosting me,
I could quite naturally go
    gray
Just thinking of how much
    it's costing me!
— Betty Isler.

Middle-Aged Mama
I'm caught between two vocal
    femmes
Whose views grow ever
    stronger.
My daughter wants to hoist
    my hems,

My mother wants them
    longer!
— Irene Warsaw.

Attention, Annie Oakley!
Tent dresses have yet
To prove for my money
That a woman can get
A man with a gunny.
— Cliff Mackay.

Daffynitions
    Fashion show: frocks trot.
— Daisy Brown.

    Face cream: Goop
therapy.
— Mary Lee Sauermann.

    Cosmetics: Crease paint.
— Raymond J. Cvikota.

    Nightgown: nap sack.

Contradiction
Milady will scream at a little
    field mouse,
Or a snake that is trespassing
    near the house.
She'll jump at a moth as it
    flits at the light
And a spider will cause her
    to take off in fright.
So, can you explain how
    she'll happily choose
To be decked out in lizard
    skin handbag and shoes?
— Vicki L. Boggs.

Fashions

Saving Grace
From these new styles
I read no moral disaster,
Girls dressed in miniskirts
Are able to run faster.
—Ruth Schenley.

Whole Cloth
I'm one of those chaps who
    unfailingly botches
When buying his clothes just
    by looking at swatches.
The pattern and texture I
    thought would look
    charming
Emerge, custom tailored, as
    something alarming;
For judging from inches I
    cannot envision
The yards of material with
    much precision
And though there are others
    who somehow compute it,
I start and I end this game
    rather ill-suited!
—Bern Sharfman.

Wrong Size
I view bikinis
With contempt,
And furthermore,
I'm slacks exempt.
—Lenore Eversole Fisher.

Biased View
[*"The Midis are Coming,
So Knees Are Going—
Beautiful People Already
Have Lowered Hems to Mid-
Calf—" WSJ headline.*]

The mini-skirt was all the
    rage,
And now we have the midi;
The way these hemlines rise
    and fall
Could make leg-watchers
    giddy!
—G. Sterling Leiby.

Knee Knocker
I think that I shall never see
A bone as homely as the
    knee,
And unless those hemlines
    fall,
I may not look at girls at all!
—R. E. Christiansen.

Neck and Neck
The filly once wore
Beads and baubles galore,
But now it's the stallion
Who sports the medallion.
—G. Sterling Leiby.

Self Protection
A woman who wears
sensible shoes probably
doesn't expect to be swept
off her feet.
—Franklin P. Jones.

Foothold
Leisure suits are moving out.
Narrow ties are coming back.
Hair styles are getting shorter
And vests are again on track.

I view these changes in
    vogue
Without ranting or raving;
It's proof that I'll yet wear
The spats that I've been
    saving.
—Arnold J. Zarett.

Suitable Garb
[*"Leisure suits are out—"*
—WSJ item]
Another style that didn't last!
One question, please, then I
    must run:
With the leisure suit a thing
    of the past,
Will there be more work
    getting done?
—G. Sterling Leiby.

Clothes Call
Arabs wear a loose burnoose,
In America sweaters are tight;
Parkas are par for Polar
    ploys,
For Malaysians, sarongs are
    right

In Britain, suspenders are
    braces;
In Ireland, a cobeen's a hat;
I can't recall what East
    Indians wear—
Sari about that!
—George O. Ludcke.

Altered Ego
Though clothes may make
    the man (or woman)—
Many people swear it's true—

Fashions

I'm shocked at garments
  salesclerks show me,
Stating firmly: "This is you!"
        —Rosemarie Williamson.

Suits Me!

Those pants with the flare at
  the bottom,
I'm glad that at last I have
  got 'em.
And here's what I happily
  muse on:
I can put on my pants with
  my shoes on.
          —Richard Armour.

Head Tax

The death of men's hats
  across the nation
May be due to the hat check
  operation;
It isn't the cost of that new
  chapeau,
But its parking fee wherever
  you go!
          —G. O. Ludcke.

Liberation Supreme!

  ["*Woeful midi skirt
retailers say the lower the
hem the lower the sales—
WSJ item.*]
At fashion czars (and
  physicists)
The girls this year have
  scoffed—
For when the midi skirt came
  down,
The mini stayed aloft!
          —Judy Michaels.

Fads

Fads

Hindsight
Of course you could always
   write a book,
But there is a method that's
   quicker
To proclaim your opinion to
   the world—
Put it on a bumper sticker!
         —George O. Ludke.

Observation Point
    Fads prove that youth will
be swerved.
         —Frank Tyger.

New Fad?
I refuse to mow the lawn,
I'm giving it a pass;
If others have pet rocks,
I'll have pet grass.
         —Gil Stern.

Looking Back
    The growing popularity of
genealogy suggests that most
of us just can't believe that
there isn't someone in our
past who amounted to
something.
         —Robert Fuoss.

Zoo-diac
A Taurus is too apt to shoot
   the bull,
A Leo is no gentle tabby;
There's something fishy about
   Pisces,
And a Cancer is too darn
   crabby.

There's often a sting to a
   Scorpio,
If you cross a Capricorn,
   there's trouble;
An Aquarius always waters
   things down,
And, by Gemini, you'll see
   double.
         —George O. Ludcke.

Horror Scope?
I sometimes wonder about
   human nature—
Its incomprehensible design—
When people can't tell you
   their blood type,
But always know their
   astrological sign!
         —Ruth M. Walsh.

Apace
This is the "with it"
   generation.
No one, I'm sure, could
   doubt it.
And what "it" is, I do not
   know,
But I could do without it.
         —Richard Armour.

Gift Hoarse
    Classified ad in a local
paper: Practically brand-new
CB Radio at fraction of
original cost. Present owner
all talked-out.
         —Edward Stevenson.

Fashion Footnote
    [*"Electric socks get more
popular."—WSJ item.*]
Electric socks deservedly
Are gaining popularity;
And as a footnote, one might
   add,
They're more than just a
   current fad.
         —Henry Barton.

Blank Expression
    Pity the people who have
no opinion—for they shall go
through life without a bumper
sticker.
         —Gil Stern.

Smile!
The way they keep nagging
   me, "Have a happy day!"
Is enough to drive my
   happiness away.
         —Colleen Stanley Bare.

So He Thinks
Upon the elbows of his coat
Are leather patches, you will
   note,
And in his mouth he has a
   pipe
On which he puffs. He is the
   type
Who needs no more. These
   are effectual
In making him an intellectual.
         —Richard Armour.

Fads

Antiques, Limited
Collectors searching for
   antiques
Are pouncing happily
On lamps, stoves, bottles,
   furniture,
Rings, postcards, pottery—

Even the rusted weathervane
On many a weathered
   steeple.
Anything old is in demand—
Excepting, of course, people.
         —E. B. de Vito.

The Kindness That Kills
Before morning ends
I look haggard and gray;
I'm being destroyed
By: "Have a good day!"
         —Arnold J. Zarett.

Crabgrass?
Like many people today
I've been seeking my ethnic
   seeds;
But I'm afraid that my
   version of "Roots"
Could only be called
   "Weeds!"
         —Ruth M. Walsh.

Wave Lengths
    CB—It may stand for
citizens band, but sometimes
when you listen to it for a
long time it stands for
"constant bore."
         —Ron Rich.

Rapid Transit
I've never studied speed
   reading,
Though it's one of today's
   rages.
My method is even faster—
I just keep skipping pages.
         —Arnold J. Zarett.

The Flip Side
    The only way to describe
teenagers who love ear-
shattering music: the Decibels'
Advocates.
         —Shelby Friedman.

Gentle Reminder
    ["*Revival of interest in
geneaolgy is taking place on
a nationwide scale.*"—*News
note*]
When you start to examine
   the family tree
You're bound to be taking
   chances—
Not so much on what you'll
   find at the roots
As what's apt to fly out of
   some branches!
         —George O. Ludcke.

Candid Comment
    Fashion designers live off
the fad of the land.
         —Frank Tyger.

The Last Word
So you think you've been
   gabbing, or yakking, or
   jawing,
Or chewing the fat, when not
   hemming or hawing.
Well, let me inform you, your
   cant has been napping—
What you have been doing
   (I'll clue you) is "rapping"!
         —G. Sterling Leiby.

Postal Pains

"Pretend you're scared—it makes him feel so good."

Gourmet Postage?
To help the price raise
Seem less vicious,
Couldn't they make
The stickum delicious?

I'm not asking the Post Office
Any other favors
Except, please, could we have
A choice of flavors?
    —Ruth Stewart Schenley.

Wrong Priority
The mails are peculiar,
The mails get me miffed:
The letters are slow—
But the bills are all swift!
    —Robert Gordon.

Stamp of Disapproval
Commemorative postage
    stamps,
I muse, while one I'm
    sticking,
Cost more, I'd think,
For paper, ink—
And take a lot more licking!
    —Richard Armour.

Postal Plea
The mailing lists that have
    my name!
A check from me's their
    common aim,
I wish that I could clear the
    decks
And get on lists that send
    me checks!
    —Elinor K. Rose.

Postal Pains

Occupant's Protest
Judging from the junk that's
    sent
To me, why, by the bale,
I guess that I must represent,
Alas, a third-class male!
                    —Bert Kruse.

Junk Mail
I'm an ardent friend of
    wildlife
And a well-known stamp
    collector;
And I'm a candidate, it
    seems,
For a brand new film
    projector.

I'm a friend of homeless
    orphans
And it certainly looks
Like I'm a favorite prospect
For a set of reference books.

I'm a preferred credit risk
For clocks and radios and
    skis,
But, to be honest with you,
I'm not any one of these.
It's just that I'm addressed
    with
All these varied salutations
On a host of unrequested
Direct mail solicitations!
                    —G. O. Ludcke.

Daily Winner
Though unlucky at lotteries
    and raffles,
In the morning, often as not,
I'll open my mailbox and
    find,

Once again I've hit the
    junkpot.
                    —Edward F. Dempsey.

Spaced Out
Commemorative stamps it
    seems
Are getting larger yearly,
And on an envelope that's
    small
I find I'm cramped severely.

If they get even larger still
(And this I oft digress on),
They very soon won't leave
    me room
For writing the address on.
                    —Richard Armour.

Postal Paradox
Neither snow nor rain nor
    heat
Nor any change of season
Stay these couriers from their
    appointed rounds—
So there must be another
    reason.
                    —Ruth M. Walsh.

Eliminate the Middleman!
Each morning my mail is
    cluttered with junk,
Most of it never gets read.
I'm thinking of sending in
    changes of address,
Listing my trash man instead!
                    —John Coulter.

Breaking Point
I send for every free offer,
Yet it seems my debt
    enlarges,
To the point where I'm going
    broke,
From mailing and handling
    charges.
                    —Edward F. Dempsey.

Letter Bugged
    If first class postage rates
go any higher, we suggest the
picture of Jesse James should
be shown on it.
                    —George E. Bergman.

Contents Noted
Not worth the stamp or even
    the glue on it
Is the average letter with
    postage due on it.
                    —Richard Armour.

Domino Effect
I'd send a check to the
    worthy cause—
But the gnawing feeling
    persists
That, if I do, my name will
    be placed
On five more mailing lists.
                    —George O. Ludcke.

Auto Suggestions

"You better take a closer look at that sign."

All About Autos

When mankind's aching feet
  got sore
From treading rocks and
  gravel,
It cleverly invented cars
To ease its mode of travel.

Among the blessings flowing
  from
This epochal solution
Were traffic jams and parking
  fines
And much more air pollution.

By dodging all those rushing
  cars,
Pedestrians grew nimble,
But most of all, now mankind
  had
A brand new status symbol.
　　　　　Robert Lovett.

Taking Sides

The sides of my car have
  scratches and dents,
Caused by other cars failing
  to stop,
As I look at my car,
So many there are,
I'd say I've a bumper crop.
　　　　　Richard Armour.

Car Dolor

Three bolts are loose, It
  rattles,
The wheels are out of line,
The lights are out of focus;
The engine has a whine.
The paint, in spots, is peeling,

Auto Suggestions

Its defects can't be hid.
Why don't I get a new car?
I'm sad to say, I did.
—Ellie Womack.

Inheritance Tracks
By studying my car's bumpers
You can tell where it has
  been;
The canyons, caverns,
  mountains
And dude ranches it has
  seen.

The car is stuck with stickers
Of places all over the land;
People gaze at me in envy—
But I got it second-hand.
—Arnold J. Zarett.

Flashcast
One of the major
automobile manufacturers is
said to be working on a
fantastic new option. It's an
electronic message board that
permits you to change
bumper copy instantly.
—Robert Fuoss.

Universal Tests
Each man differs from the
  next
In the goals to which he
  aspires,
But car buyers from every
  walk of life
Slam the doors and kick the
  tires.
—George O. Ludcke.

False Alarm
"I've discovered oil on our
property," a woman told her
husband when he came home
from work.

"Why, that's great!" he
cried. "We'll finally be able to
get a new car!"

"My feeling is that we'd
better get the old car fixed,"
sighed the wife, "That's where
the oil seems to be coming
from."
—Harold Helfer.

Motor Matter
Our car, which starts
  reluctantly,
Will stutter, spit and cough;
The thing's confused; it runs,
  enthused,
As soon as I shut it off.
—Dick Emmons.

Wheels of Regress
I just sent the last of
My car payments in.
I swore that I'd do it or bust.
And now that my vehicle's
All free and clear,
It's turned to a bucket of
  rust.
—Joseph P. Waitz.

Whodunit
Soaring insurance rates
Are really a shame;
It may be no-fault,
But someone's to blame!
—Arnold J. Zarett.

What, No Nurses?
Grim men in white with
  clipboards
Conferring in muted tone;
The nervous husband pacing
In the corridor alone.
The patient being examined—
A scene out of Dr. Kildare?
Nope, diagnostic consultation
At the clinic for auto repair!
—G. O. Ludcke.

Auto Logic
It's no wonder, so many cars
  are recalled;
Now when you stop to
  consider
They average ten-thousand
  parts apiece—
Each supplied by the lowest
  bidder!

Vengeance Ahead
There's one good thing
about the trend toward
compact cars. If they
continue to get smaller,
pedestrians will soon be
able to strike back.
—Robert Fuoss.

Urban Dwellers

"Since the barn was torn down I've
become a condominium owl."

Apt-ly Named
When leasing an apartment,
I thought that "high rise"
    meant
A description of the building
But I know now it's the rent!
                —Charlotte Koss.

Name of the Game
    Now that families are living
in condominiums, shouldn't
the housing for swinging
singles be called
pandemoniums?
                —Daisy Brown.

Daffynitions
    Urban renewal: Shack
absorber.

    Tenant strike: the path of
lease resistance.
                —Raymond J. Cvikota.

    Demolition: broken
premises.
                —Robert Fitch.

The Living End
I view the world ahead
And picture a millennium
In which the Noah's Ark to
    come
Will be co-op or
    condominium.
                —Arnold J. Zarett.

Urban Dwellers

Urban Blurb
The streets of your city,
I'll make a deduction,
Are all over-crowded
Or under construction.
—Nova Trimble Ashley.

Pillow Talk?
To an urban man, a
sleeping bag is the unkindest
cot of all.
—Raymond J. Cvikota.

Strung Out
["No clothing shall be hung
outside on a clothesline or
similar apparatus. . . ."—
Clause from an apartment
house lease]
To keep the environs looking
regal,
Clotheslines are declared
illegal.
Clean linen may not flutter
free
From sill or roof of Building
Three,
Although you'll find there's no
taboo
On linen, soiled, in public
view!
—Joyce Carlile LaMers.

Spreading the Stealth
They speak of "crime in the
streets"—
And this without doubt is
true.

But I'd like your attention
While something I mention:
There's crime on the
sidewalks, too.
—Richard Armour.

Forced Order
The trouble with living in a
studio apartment is there's no
place to put anything except
where it belongs.
—Anna Herbert.

Rent and Rave
Oh, for the good old days
When things were in the
groove;
When you could get landlords
to fix anything
Just by threatening to move!

Census
Many people who leave the
farm to go to the city are
folks who are trying to
make enough money to go
back to the farm.
—Ola Beavers.

The Porn is Green

Smut Glut
["Pornographers are
singing the blues—'Our
customers get tired of seeing
the same thing week after
week.'"—WSJ news item]
If you've seen one you've
seen them all
Is the way some viewers
dismiss it—
For what do you do for an
encore
After you've been explicit?
—E. V. Girand.

Don't Push!
The censors may click their
tongues in disdain
Over what they call
pornographic,
But when something lewd has
to be reviewed,
They create quite a jam with
their traffic.
—G. O. Ludcke.

Hall of Ill-Fame
People are talking about
the clever pornographer who
became a legend in his slime.
—Shelby Friedman.

Daffynitions
X-rated movie profits:
pornucopia.
—Shelby Friedman.

Early stag films: original
cine.
—Stuart Citrin.

The Porn is Green

X-rated movie: strip
rniming.
— Henry Barton.

For the Birds?
With outdoor viewings of X-
rated films,
At drive-ins, outdoor theaters
and such,
Perhaps the birds and bees
will have
An opportunity to learn
something from us.
— R. M. Walsh.

Shelf Effacement
Sign in the window of a
side-street book store: "Special
Sale on All Pornography. Dirt
Cheap."
— Bob de Luryea.

"You're investigating pornography and I'm stuck with
wheat prices."

VIII SHIFTING LIFE STYLES

"I can't understand it. There's been only bad news for
the last fifty years and yet we're still here."

Mores—Changing and Otherwise

"This is a real tough section of town!"

Daffynitions
Morality: knowing all there is to no.

—Frank Tyger.

It's a Gift
When your're given a present
That's just what you want,
And very expensive,
The sort that you flaunt,

I defy you to say,
And no words am I mincing,
"You shouldn't have done it"
And sound quite convincing.

—Richard Armour.

Open Hand
For giving instead of
    receiving,
I favor casting my vote;
Not only is it more blessed
But it saves a thank-you note.

—May Richstone.

Sad Statistic
One of today's riddles is how, in a world growing smaller and a population growing larger, people are drifting farther apart.

—Dodge City Globe.

Center of Interest
No conversation bores me if
The topic's one of three:
My children, or the work I
do,
Or just—let's face it—me!

—Lester A. Sobel.

Mores—Changing and Otherwise

Blankety-Blank
Though I have known your
name for years,
My memory of it disappears
Or stutters to some dismal
end
When I present you to a
friend.
—Ing Smith.

Good Listener
In the art of conversation,
I'm just born to lose,
All I do is sit around
And admire the views.
—Maurice Seitter.

Name Tag
A Hollywood ham was
injured in an auto crash.
When the police searched his
wallet for identification papers
they found this note: "In case
of accident please call all
three networks."
—Robert Fuoss.

Foot of Clay
I never touch the bubbly stuff,
Nor even yet the foamy;
I covet no one else's wife,
I'm strictly home-sweet-homey.

I never touch tobacco,
LSD or marijuana,
And even feel a guilty twinge
When steaming in the sauna.

I love my neighbor as myself,
Or maybe even more,
And wish the Ten

Commandments
Had been multiplied by four.

I never curse or frequent
dens
Iniquitous and fleshly,
And seldom think an evil
thought
Of anyone especially.

In short—and this is what I
find
So very gratifying—
I've only got one little fault,
One teensy foible: Lying!
—William Corbin McGraw.

Tolerance Note
We should look kindly on
those people who disagree
with us. After all, they're
entitled to their stupid
opinions!
—C. McClure.

Show Motion
Some people think that
just because they are on the
move they are going places.
—H. E. Martz.

Reminder
Two men were lunching
together, and one had
difficulty in keeping his eyes
off their beautiful waitress.
"What a gorgeous girl!" he
exclaimed.
"Six kids," muttered his
friend.

"She's got six children?"
"No," replied the chum
gently, "you have!"
—Pru Pratt.

Candidly Shrinking
"Do you want my honest
opinion?"
People ask. I say, "Yes," for
I'm curious.
So they give me their honest
opinion,
And I—well, I'm always
furious!
—Richard Armour.

Sports Item
Those who drop the ball
are usually the ones who
complain about the way it
bounces.
—H. E. Martz.

Daffynition
Conscience: Faults alarm.
—Dana Robbins.

**Thoughts While Wool
Gathering**
People are like sheep, they
say—
And not entirely in jest.
But life's a gambol, anyway,
So maybe it's for the best.
—Suzanne Douglass.

Mores—Changing and Otherwise

Slow Talker
Some folks are so glib
That they can ad lib—
Refusals they make with
    finesse;
Whenever I grope,
And try to say nope,
I find I've already said yes!
                —W.J. Cronenberger.

Note Worthy
No matter what you say or
    do,
No matter what folks say to
    you,
Discretion says that it's much
    better
Not to put it in a letter.
                —Anna Herbert.

The Unsuspecting
    The trouble with remaining
calm these days is that
people suspect you don't
know what's going on.
                —Franklin P. Jones.

Small Request
While wealth would be great,
So would beauty and
    brilliance,
But all I'm asking from fate
Nowadays is resilience!
                —May Richstone.

Tale End
I'm prepared to listen at
    length

To details of an epic sort
Whenever I hear some say:
"To make a long story short
    —"!
                —Arnold J. Zarett.

Divester's System
A little gambling now and
    then
Is relished by the wisest men;
The wisest men, of course,
    are they
Who own the joints where
    gamblers play.
                —Dal Devening.

Daffynition
    Bachelor's apartment: a
site for soirees.
                —Raymond J. Cvikota.

Instant Information
    Another kind of pessimist:
Someone who can't hear
opportunity knock because
he's busy knocking
opportunity!
                —Dana Robbins.

Social Note
    America is where you can
become a blueblood simply by
having more greenbacks.
                —Bill Copeland.

Smoke Screen
When does a man look half
    so wise

As when he's puffing on his
    pipe,
And leaning back and
    shutting eyes?
You'd swear this guy's the
    thinking type!
Yet if you could but read his
    mind
As he just puffs, eyes narrow
    slits,
You'd find his pipe is just a
    blind
To stall for time to gather
    wits!
                —Jerry Cowle.

Moral Examples
I sometimes shudder when I
    count the list
Of all the moral lessons we'd
    have missed
If Robert Bruce had simply
    killed the spider,
Or Paul Revere had been a
    lousy rider,
Or Androcles had brashly
    kicked the lion,
Or William Tell had shot his
    doughty scion,
Or if—and here my
    shuddering is treble—
Demosthenes had strangled
    on a pebble.
Without those fine examples
    to hold onto,
Just think what moral dogs
    we might have gone to!
                —Georgie Starbuck Galbraith.

Mores—Changing and Otherwise

Success Formula
The climb to the top
requires a wife to tell the
man what to do—and a
secretary to do it.
—Duane Dewlap.

Note to the Self-Righteous
A halo is a fine thing to
wear, but it's been known to
slip and become a noose.
—Silas Shay.

On the Jump
The way many people
Jump to conclusions,
It's a wonder there aren't
More cuts and contusions.
—Richard Armour.

Quirk Analysis
Most people today are
tolerant to a fault. What they
can't tolerate is virtue.
—Edith Ogutsch.

Who Said That?
I never think before I speak,
My words I do not weigh;
I find it more exciting when
I don't know what I'll say.
—Maurice Seitter.

Temptation
I'd never give it
Another glance
If I could be sure
Of a second chance!
—Thomas Usk.

False Colors
Sometimes what we
admire as a virtue is nothing
more than lack of
opportunity.
Robert Fuoss.

To The Manner Borne
Emily Post was the arbiter
On mores and manners,
forsooth—
One might almost call her
A veritable fountain of couth.
—R. M. Walsh.

Toothfully Speaking
What, you ask, is a smile?
I can tell you in very small
space:
It's when you feel good all
over
But show it in only one
place.
—Richard Armour.

Pony Tale
"Horse Sense" might be
summarized as knowing when
to say "neigh."
—Rosemarie Williamson.

Up Front
A tactless person is
someone who says what
everyone is thinking.
—Lucille S. Harper.

Suggestion Blocks
Most folks accept good
advice—if it doesn't interfere
with their plans.
—Paul Harwitz.

Daffynition
Celebrity Register: most
vaunted list.

Emulation
Laugh and the world laughs
with you
Is a saying that's probably
true.
But truer still, I have noticed:
Yawn and others yawn, too.
—Richard Armour.

Please, Not Everybody!
In love for our fellow mortals
Gladly would we bask—
But why must some of them
make it
Such an impossible task?
—May Richstone.

Beginning of Wisdom
I used to say Yes, No,
Certainly—
With never a doubtful lapse;
But the longer I live, the
oftener
I say Possibly, Maybe,
Perhaps.
—May Richstone.

Mores—Changing and Otherwise

Home-Bound
A guy who rates No. 1
As a conversational bore
Can spoil a beautiful evening
Keeping his feat in the door.
— Maurice Seitter.

Fitting Accolade
He who in public shows no
    dread
Of correcting another's
    grammar
Surely deserves a pat on the
    head,
Preferably with a hammer.
— Georgie Starbuck Galbraith.

The Clove that Cleaves
    [*"More Americans are
eating more garlic."*—WSJ
news item.]
Another crisis in our nation?
Some new source of
    alienation?
No, only garlic, the latest
    craze—
Now it's entering its salad
    days.
A paradoxical condiment,
It causes pleasure and then
    dissent.

Yet we can solve this little
    matter
If we agree to eat and
    scatter.
So let us share this
    flavorsome flora
And allow ourselves margin
    for aura.
— Arch Napier.

Not Guilty
It might be great to be rich,
It might be nice to be
    famous,
But still it's not so bad in the
    crowd
Where nobody can blame us.
— Maurice Seitter.

For the Birds
I've never heard a pigeon
    speak.
'Twould make my spine all
    tinglish.
And yet, like you, I many
    times
Have heard of pigeon English.
— Richard Armour.

Female Complaint
The male who makes passes
And murmurs words flirty
Turns out to be married
And well over thirty.
— Robert Gordon.

Truth Capsule
    It's hard to keep a chip
on your shoulder when
somebody's shaking your
hand.
— Franklin P. Jones.

Overview
Each of us is wired
In a different way:
Some people sleep little,
While others doze all day.

Some are always pressured,
While others feel untaxed,
Some may climb the walls,
While others are relaxed.

Some must get ahead,
While others do not care,
Some buy stocks in blocks,
While others like one share.

Some will take your word,
While others will doubt it.
Some ignore all this—
While others write about it.
— Arnold J. Zarett.

Snob Story
    The son of a successful,
selfmade manufacturer became
engaged to the daughter of
an equally wealthy but socially
prominent family.
    When the two sets of
parents met, the social lion
barely disguised his roar of
disapproval. "I know your son
is a student at Harvard, and
our daughter goes to Radcliffe
—just as her mother and
grandmother did. But I'm
afraid I didn't catch the name
of your alma mater. Did you
go to Harvard?"
    "No, I didn't," came the
soft reply, "but at least 500
of my two thousand employes
did."
— Murray Cohen.

Mores—Changing and Otherwise

COCHRAN:

"One sees such candor now-a-days!"

Plastic Praise?
Flattery is pleasant.
We all enjoy its grace.
But it's a bit like warming
    one's self
At an artificial fireplace.
           —Ruth M. Walsh.

Mutual Assent
Anybody who asks for
advice probably only wants to
know how well you agree
with him.
           —Franklin P. Jones.

Energy Crisis
A discussion that gets out of
    hand
And ends up in a fight
Will generate a lot of heat
But won't shed any light.
           —Charlotte Koss.

Social Item
Courtesy is a quality that
enables a person to stand
quietly in line when a boor
gets the best table.

Capsule Philosophy
If a man isn't content
with what he has, he should
at least be grateful for what
he's escaped.

Lighting Up
The spotlight of notoriety
Increases each day and hour.
Getting famous and rich in

Mores—Changing and Otherwise

the spotlight
Depends on its scandal-power.
　　　　　　—Richard Armour.

Borrowed Drama
Headlines are meant to grab
　　you,
Especially the ones that're
　　bolder;
But none claim more
　　attention
Than those glimpsed over a
　　shoulder.
　　　　—Patricia Skarry Rutter.

Mechanized
Man seems to need
The age of speed
To help disaster
Happen faster.
　　　　　　—Paul Armstrong.

Pathetic Case
　　A man explained why he
steadfastly refused to purchase
life insurance. "When I die, I
want it to be a sad day for
everyone."

View From the Bottom
He's known as a man of
　　means,
But people are somewhat
　　confused,
They know of the means he
　　has
But wonder what means he
　　used.
　　　　　　—Richard Armour.

Who, Me?
Infallibility, it appears,
Is not part of man's lot;
To err is only human—
To admit the error is not.
　　　　　　—George O. Ludcke.

Envy
Envy is the art,
And it's very well known
Of counting another's
　　blessings
Instead of one's own.
　　　　　　—R.M. Walsh.

Daffynition
　　Social climbing:gilt by
association.
　　　　　　—Honey Greer.

Waiting Game
I'm not one to bear ill will,
I have never held a grudge.
Forgive and forget, I say,
And from this rule I don't
　　budge
From desires to get even
I seem to have immunity—
Unless, of course, I find
A splendid opportunity!
　　　　　　—Arnold J. Zarett.

Bad News
Trying to break it gently has
Seldom succeeded. In palace
　　or hut
Few words are as alarming as
"I don't want to alarm you,
　　but…"!
　　　　　　—Ethel Jacobson.

Daffynition
　　Tact: tongue in check.
　　　　　　—Arnold Glasow.

Timing Tip
　　Punctuality is the art of
guessing how late the other
fellow will be.

Being at the 60s and 70s

"Hey, Dad, what war was this?"

Child Care
A well-adjusted youngster is one who can play happily at the Day Care Center while his parents attend a seminar on the declining quality of family life.
—Robert Fuoss.

Saigon Sigh
The war news never seems
   to end,
(And most of it is glum),
While I don't know about
   you, friend,
I'm getting Viet numb.
—Dick Emmons.

Generation Jape
A father was berating his daughter for her slovenly appearance. "You modern day kids are so messy and unkempt, it boggles the mind to even think about your numerous other deficiencies. Why, just look at your hair! It looks like a mop!"

"Gee, daddy," said the girl innocently, "what's a mop?"

Daffynitions
Student militants: Dean agers.
—Robert Fitch.

Contraband: Music of Rock and Roll Groups.
—Raymond J. Cvikota.

Being at the 60s and 70s

Discotheque: Spinal
wresting place.
—John B. Dromey.

The Over-Thirties Strike Back!
"Kids are much smarter
today,"
I always hear everyone say,
But I simply don't see the
grand fuss.
If they're so acute,
Worldly-wise and astute,
How come they don't
understand us?
—Arnold J. Zarett.

Prodigy's Problem
Perhaps the cruelest thing
a parent can do nowadays is
to push a bright child through
school too fast. What if he
arrives at college too young
to grow a beard?
—Wichita Eagle.

Generation Revisited
Oh, long-haired, moustached,
bearded one,
Some short-haired, shaven,
father's son,
You won't like what I have
to say,
That you resemble a past
day,
Which you may find quite a
bother;
You look just like your great
grandfather.
—Colleen Stanley Bare.

Second Time Around
Re-runs are popular on T.V.,
But a new re-run now
abounds:
Making a second pot of
coffee
Over the used grounds.
—Ruth M. Walsh.

It Had to Happen:
Someone's introducing a new
perfume with the nostalgic
aroma of coffee.
—Arnold Glasow.

Fashion Note
Sign on a construction
project: "All men on the job
must wear safety hats
regardless of their political
opinion."
—Herm Albright.

Rock Lullaby
Rock-a-bye baby, asleep in the
cot,
Don't bug your mama, she's
smoking her pot;
Daddy is busily doing his
Thing,
Whatever that is (He's been
loafing since spring!)
Rock-a-bye baby, and get in
the groove.
Maybe some day you will
grow up to prove
That mod-style parents who
simply hang loose

Can still do okay by their
little papoose.
—Ann R. Franco.

From an Old Grad
Attack if you must your
president.
Tear down the halls of
reason.
But spare, I beseech you, the
football coach.
He's having a winning season.
—Robert Fuoss.

Relevant Question
He reads about the campus
strife
And ponders on such riotous
life;
Perhaps he's just a fuddy-
duddy,
But when do college students
study?
—Elinor K. Rose.

Classtrophobia
Take a look at the educational
scene
And campuses rent and rioty.
How Marx would rejoice as
our schools close down
And we have a classless
society.
—Richard Armour.

At Decade's End
The decade had us all
appalled:
The Savage Sixties it's been

Being at the 60s and 70s

called.
Oh, may the next one on the scene
Be termed the Seventies Serene?
　　　　—C. Cushman Lee.

Personal Contact
In colleges today the new twist
For students making the scene,
Is not getting on the dean's list.
It's merely getting the dean.
　　　　—Leonard Dittell.

Demonstration Note
It's a fact that there are militant students even among those taking correspondence courses. One young man we know recently beat up his mailman.
　　　　—Ida Rose.

For the Record
With neither hawk nor dove I'd
Want to be compared.
If I must need be classified,
Just file me under "Scared."
　　　　—John D. Swan.

Combat Training
The young demonstrators who just plop down so that nobody can get through are only employing a technique they learned earlier in front of their TV sets.

A Gruesome Outlook
Now drugs are out, Gurus are in;
According to statistics,
New darlings of the campus are
These transcendental mystics.
Explore your inner self, they say,
Rewards are rich and real;
While that may be, they're not for me,
Their creed lacks sect's appeal!
　　　　—Bob Herz.

Updated, in Living Color
It's clear the prude is outmoded now.
The many changes in modern morals
Demand that the oldster must learn how
To be broad-minded, avoiding quarrels.
So when the girls are scantily clad
And the humor is much too brash and sexy,
I'm very tolerant and, I'll add,
I'm often purple with apoplexy.
　　　　—George Starbuck Galbraith.

Pre-Party Briefing
Dear husband, let's keep our party quiet.
In launching a conversational gambit,
Don't even so much as mention riot—
And try to avoid the Vietnam bit.
Let peace prevail at our festive discussions,
Lest guests cut loose like vociferous thugs,
Steer clear of the Red Chinese and the Russians,
The hippies and psychedelic drugs.
Just what free speech can your speech be free on?
Well, skip the Supreme Court's Justice Warren
And stick to subjects all men agree on:
The cost of living and Sophia Loren.
　　　　—George Starbuck
　　　　　　　　Galbraith.

Language Batterer
My efforts to communicate
Are really quite a struggle.
To keep my language up to date,
I have to switch and juggle.
Since "meaningful relationships"
Can be derailed by verbal slips,
I'm "disadvantaged," never poor,

Being at the 60s and 70s

I don't get older, I "mature";
I'm not disgruntled, granite-
    crusted,
I'm merely somewhat
    "maladjusted,"
And when I howl and beat
    my breast,
I'm not rambunctious, I
    "protest"!
I'll own I'm not the type to
    squawk,
But it would not surprise me
If wrestling with this double-
    talk
Should simply "finalize" me!
            —George Starbuck Galbraith.

Message to Milton
God's ways to man you
    justified
With apostolic zeal for truth;
Take pity on us, come again,
And justify the ways of youth.
            —Sam Hudson.

Drafty
    After threatening to burn
his draft card, the timid
graduate student finally
changed his mind. He boiled
it instead.

Measured Opinion
    ["Going Metric Poses
Problems for U.S."—
newspaper headline.]
It may be hard for mom to
    adjust
To strawberries by the liter,

And dad will resist taking
    measurements
By the silly millimeter.
The change to the metric
    system
Is causing some speculation
On how long it will take the
    nation
To complete its metriculation.
            —G. O. Ludcke.

Adventure Story
    Now that we've
demonstrated man can walk
on the moon it's time we
proved he can walk down
Main Street after dark.
            —Robert Fuoss.

And So It Goes
As the Sunset Legislation
Sinks slowly beneath the Hill
We're happy to learn that the
    Shortfall
Won't result in Overkill.
With Zero-based Budgeting in
    vogue
And The Transition all
    completed,
We can now relax with our
    Income Tax
(Expletive Deleted!)
            —George O. Ludcke.

Reduced Ratio
Now that granny's buying
    mini skirts,
The generation gap seems
    small:

Junior has her steel-rimmed
    specs
And sister wears her shawl.
            —Lorraine Byman.

Fine Feathered Trend
MuuMuus, track shoes,
Turtlenecks for either sex;
Long skirts, T-shirts,
Jackets with vents, dresses
    called "tents"
Riding boots, patchwork suits,
Wooden clogs, safari togs
Culottes, ascots,
Shoes labeled "walkers," caps
    for deerstalkers;
String ties, caftans, capes and
    jeans—
In these America is now
    attired;
So I can't help wondering
    what it means—
The stipulation: Proper Dress
    Required!
            —Rosemarie Williamson.

Family Portrait
    If you see a picture of a
group of long-haired dudes all
dressed up in fancy clothes,
they're either rock musicians
or signers of the Declaration
of Independence.
            —Robert Fuoss.

Daffynitions
    Disco dancing; Sacroiliact.
            —Honey Greer.

Being at the 60s and 70s

Armstrong and Aldrin: The awed couple.
—Ralph Noel.

Missile gap: Science friction.
—Raymond J. Cvikota.

Thumbing a ride: hitchcraft.
—Al Graham.

Drug traffic: Stupor market.
—Daisy Brown.

Modern Education
Sending gals to men's schools
Will not be their undoing;
They may not pursue learning
But they'll surely learn
pursuing.
—Sarah C. Neumark.

Social Change
South of the border the news
is horrendous;
The coffee price increase is
simply stupendous,
And parties that used to be
B.Y.O.B.
Will shortly be switching to
B.Y.O.C.
—Jane Herald.

No Show
No more demonstrations,
please,
With sign or rock or gun.
No more need to
demonstrate—
We know how it is done.
—Richard Armour.

Star Cross
I'd like this dawning Age of
Aquarius
Much better if things weren't
so darned precarious;
In fact, if you want my
candid reaction,
There's already too much
Zodiaction.
As for the gurus of astrology
—
They owe this planet an
apology!
—G. O. Ludcke.

Hair

Zoo Story
The girl's father regarded
the long-haired youth who
had come over to spend the
evening. "Tell me, son," he
said finally, "is that your own
hair—or are you traveling
under an assumed mane?"
—Lane Olinghouse.

With It and Without
"Roger wasn't even a
successful hippie," the young
man's father mused sadly. "At
twenty, he began to lose his
hair."
—Edward Stevenson.

Materials Progress
How coiffures change! The
bards of old
Praised girls with hair of flax
or gold;
The dames that modern poets
smile on?
Most of them have wigs of
nylon!
—Herbert Warfel.

The Defense Rests
["The average American
male spends 3,350 hours of
his life shaving."—WSJ item.]
My love for my beard
Is suddenly stronger,
Now that I can sleep
3,000 hours longer.
—Arnold J. Zarett.

Hair

Clip Joint
My days of low-priced
Haircuts are gone,
For my local barbershop
Is now a salon.
> —Edward F. Dempsey.

Modern Miracle
The dye is cast . . .
I'm blonde at last.
> —Gail Cooke.

Moral Fiber
The compliments on my new
    wig
Are more than I can bear;
I never hear such glowing
    things
When wearing my own hair.
> —Ellie Womack.

Pate Commiserate
Young men complain that
    they can't get jobs
Because of long hair today.
But if they think they have it
    tough,
They should try it with hair
    sparse and gray!
> —Ruth M. Walsh.

"We'll tolerate no short-haired malcontents in this man's army."

Nostalgia

"Ivy, where the hell are my love beads?"

Clean Forgotten

Regarding styles of hair and
    clothes
On which the young routinely
    pounce,
What has become, do you
    suppose,
Of that old saying: "Neatness
    Counts"?
          —G. Sterling Leiby.

Nostallergy

There's no sense in regretting
    the past—
Too much of our time's spent
    in yearning;
If we knew then what we
    know now,
We'd have missed all the fun
    we had learning!
          —George O. Ludcke.

Fashion Fall

    ["Brooks Brothers to End
Custom Tailoring."—News
Item.]
Gone are the clothes of
    yesteryear
That came with vest and
    britches.
Gone are the custom-tailored
    suits
That kept us all in stitches.
Gone are the artisans of yore
Who cut the cloth beyond
    compare—
Gone in a culture that prefers
Blue jeans and wash-and-
    wear.
          —Robert Gordon.

Nostalgia

Thin-ful Extravagance

When the teenaged girl returned from the market with a bag of expensive diet foods, her father was annoyed. "When I was a kid it was easy to go on a diet," he grumbled. "You just showed up for dinner two minutes late!"

—Robert Orben.

Identity Crisis

We can remember when the answer to a maiden's prayer looked a lot like Clark Gable. These days he looks a lot like the maiden.

—Lane Olinghouse.

News Report

I listen to the news upon
TV and radio,
But all the time I do, my
   friends,
I must confess I know
That neither ever will replace
The paper that it vies with—
For neither is the slightest
   use,
I've found, for swatting flies
   with.

—Richard Armour.

Gone are the Days

Son: "You've had a lot more experience than me, dad. What's your opinion?"

Bartender: "I know five cents is a lot for a glass of beer, but think of the free lunch you get with it!"

Tax collector: "No, we don't want to check your books. Your word is good enough for us."

Barber: "Want me to thin it out, on top, sir?"

Wife: "Prices are skyrocketing something awful, dear. Can you spare an extra dollar for this month?"

Me: "Well, I didn't make much money this year, but at least it's all mine."

—Frank Rose.

The Price of Pulp

The old Penny Dreadful which became the dime novel is now the Buck Ninety Awful!

—Bill Copeland.

The Harnessed Driver

["News Item: in 1968 shoulder harnesses will be required on all cars."]
In 1968 we'll wear it for
   safety's sake, of course,
But in 1908, the only one to
   wear a harness was the
   horse!

—J. E. Williams.

Surface Reflection

Each time I hope for
   something good,
And get enthusiastic,
I look around to knock on
   wood—
But all I see is plastic.

—Dick Emmons.

Nostalgia Note

You know you're old if you can remember the days when you could get the landlord to fix anything just by threatening to move.

—Paul Harwitz.

Sporting Times

In the old days a ball club that suffered from lack of customers got new ball players; today it gets a new city.

—Anna Herbert.

On the Run

Leisurely dining's
A thing of the past;
People prefer
The foods they call "fast."
They're gulping down burgers,
Hotdogs and fish
Served quickly on paper,
Not even one dish!
What's the big hurry?
It's got me perplexed—
They seem to be rushing
To where they'll eat next.

—Charlotte Koss.

Nostalgia

Throwback
Excessive use of appliances
Causes electrical power to
    fault,
And vehicular congestion
Brings traffic to a halt.

Pollution fouls the water,
Destroying what should be
    pure,
And miracles of medicine
Turn out to be no cure.

So soon I'll be buying spring
    water
And reading by candles' rays,
And wherever I go I'll be
    walking—
Hmmmm, just like the good
    old days!
                    —Arnold J. Zarett.

Remember When?
    "Lack of communication"
meant the telephone wires
were down?
    A "demonstration" was
what a Fuller Brush man
gave?
    "Hot Pants" were what
little boys got when they
misbehaved?
    A "riot" was a group of
friends playing charades?
                    —Frank Rose.

Modern Times
    A father told his son
there would be an eclipse of
the moon that night.

"Great!" exclaimed the
boy. "What channel?"
                    —Paul Harwitz.

Synthetic Note
    Ever stop to think that
the antiques of tomorrow will
all be plastic?
                    —Herm Albright.

Wrong Number
In bygone days, they had to
    crank
Those phones upon the walls:
Today we have push-button
    ease—
And the cranks are making
    the calls.
                    —Rosemarie Williamson.

Memory Lane
    Remember the good old
days, when bringing up kids
was mostly a matter of
denying them their
constitutional rights?
                    —Bob Orben.

Daffynitions
    Nostalgia: national past
time.
                    —Len Elliott.

    Nostalgia: retained
yearnings.
                    —John S. Bowdidge.

Audio Affected
It used to be that facing the
    music
Was so tough we often blew
    it.
Now it's not facing the music
    that hurts—
It's merely listening to it!
                    —Ruth M. Walsh.

Nutritional Decline
    Remember the days when
you let your child have some
chocolate if he finished his
cereal? Now, chocolate is one
of the cereals.
                    —Robert Orben.

Metric Protest
I'm one who drags his feet
    and flinches
At giving up my quarts and
    inches.
                    —Gordon Thomas.

Pointed Reminder
Modern appliances are great,
But memories of past models
    linger—
Like the first digital alarm
    clock—
(A poke in the ribs with a
    finger).

Nostalgia

Easy Does It
It used to be that "a cup of
 tea"
Meant something easy to
 take;
Later it was called "a lead
 pipe cinch";
Now it's "a piece of cake."
— George O. Ludcke.

Religion

"There must be a limit to permissiveness."

Religion

Holier Than Thou

A couple of preachers, good friends but of different denominations, often disagreed on religious issues. One day, after arguing more than usual on a theological point, one of the ministers stated: "That's all right. We'll just agree to disagree. The thing that counts is that we're both doing the Lord's work—you in your way and I in His."

—Herm Albright.

Take Your Choice

When the sexton was scolded by the townspeople for ringing the church bells so loudly on Sunday morning, he gruffly replied, "Well, if they're not coming to church, they're not going to sleep, either!"

Mixed Meanings

Fanaticism: people's attempts to change our beliefs.

Zeal: our efforts to convert them.

—Frank Rose.

Practical Parish

Said the tolerant pastor, "In our church
We follow the modern trends:
All denominations are welcome here—
Especially fives and tens."

—G. O. Ludcke.

Daffynitions

Monastery: a behave of activity.

—Raymond J. Cvikota.

Roaming evangelist: Traveling soulsman.

—Daisy Brown.

Choir practice: hymnastics.

Religious retreat: vacation with pray.

—Robert Fuoss.

Church supper: parishable goods.

—Marybelle Rollo.

Monastery: Bureau of mission persons.

—Shelby Friedman.

Hip Haiku

Blessed are the pure,
For it is clear that they shall
Inhibit the earth.

—Allen Glasser.

Foresight

It was Easter Sunday and the church was crowded to capacity. After preaching his sermon, the minister said to the congregation, "I'm delighted that so many of you came to our Easter services. And now, since I don't expect to see you for awhile, may I take this occasion to wish all of you a Merry Christmas?"

Always On Sunday

After listening to a good sermon, we either arise strengthened—or awake refreshed.

—Thomas Henry.

Double Trouble

I don't believe in reincarnation,
I want to make this clear;
I didn't even believe in it
The last time I was here!

—J. Pat Babin.

Religious Regression

Judging from the look some parishioners give you, the milk of human kindness turns sour during the battle for a parking place in the church lot.

—Bill Copeland.

Religion

Truth: Hits, Misses and Errors

Liberal View
It isn't really so hard to define Ecumenicalism. Simply, it's getting to know the opposite sects.
—Mary Lee Sauermann.

The Human Condition
Why is it easier to confess our sins than to admit our faults?
—Arnold Glasow.

"I'm the guy who tells the truth that lies somewhere in between."

Truth: Hits, Misses and Errors

Unknown Quantity
There are two groups who
  set the pace
For things most people do.
I'd love to meet them face to
  face
Before my life is through.

They're specialists in all life's
  games,
Experts on rules of play.
I only know them by their
  names:
They're—"Everyone" and
  "They."
                    —Eleanore Padnos.

Ambition Condition
The go-getters are to be
  admired
For enterprise, and yet
To me their worth depends
  somewhat
On what they go and get.
                    —Darrell Bartee.

Candid Comment
    The man who has nobody
but himself to blame will
usually think of somebody.
                    —Maurice Seitter.

Shattering Thought
Here is a thought that quite
  often
Through my head passes:
People who live in stone
  houses
Shouldn't throw glasses.
                    —Richard Armour.

Ocean Notion
I'm sure my ship will soon
  come in,
But, with no touch of rancor,
I often wonder if, by blunder,
Somebody's dropped the
  anchor?
                    —Dick Emmons.

On the Go
"Ladies first," I have heard
  for years,
And I've always been very
  polite
When opening doors or
  standing in line,
Thus doing what I thought
  right.

But lately I've come to wonder
  a bit,
And I'd like to say, if I durst,
That I've studied mortality
  tables and found
That it's men, instead, who
  go first.
                    —Richard Armour.

Memory Device
A door that's slammed and
  locked, it's funny,
Can somehow jog one's mind
Into recalling briefcase, money,
Or house keys left behind.
                    —G. Sterling Leiby.

Add This
Arithmetic is not my forte.
Subtraction or addition.
I somehow lack just what it
takes.
The brains or disposition.

Of late, though, I have
  learned a fact
That some may think a droll
  one.
It's simply this: that two half-
  truths
Don't, somehow, make a
  whole one.
                    —Richard Armour.

Clear Confusion
    It's an age of paradox
when we have mobile homes
that don't move, sports
clothes for work, work
clothing for leisure, junk food
that costs more than real
food, and sweat shirts you
wear for loafing.
                    —Arch Napier.

Where's Everybody?
The population explosion's a
  lie.
If it's not, I'll have to be
  shown
For when in trouble it seems
  that I
Always happen to be alone.
That there's too many people
  is a myth
That seems to have recently
  grown,
For when I get mugged, who
  am I with!
Outside of the mugger, alone!
And whenever I find that I
  am lost,

Truth: Hits, Misses and Errors

In broad daylight or deepest
   night,
And I need directions at any
   cost,
There's never a soul in sight.
But it's not just the loneliness
   that I mind,
For what makes me feel real
   bitter
Is that a fourth for bridge I
   can never find—
Or a New Year's eve baby-
   sitter!
        —Leonard Dittell.

Inside Story
There's nothing like writing
   the address
And sealing the envelope
   tight,
To remind you, all of a
   sudden,
Of something you wanted to
   write.
        —Stephen Schlitzer.

Final Truth
According to one cynical
newspaper reader, the only
thing he can believe in the
papers is the obituary column.

Furry Philosophy
There seems to be a
belief that some modern
dogmas are barking up the
wrong tree.
        —H. E. Martz.

Busy Signal
If someone is always "too
busy" to answer your
question, the odds are that
he doesn't know the answer.
        —Cliff Hanger.

Sweet Deceit
The worst thing about a
half-truth is that we always
seem to believe the wrong
half.
        —Robert Fuoss.

Youth Lip
They get it backwards,
The very young;
What they give us
Is cheek in tongue.
        —Bill Copeland.

All for the Best
"I gave it my best," I say
   with pride,
As if it were some sort of
   test of me.
But I must confess that I've
   nearly died
When somebody got the best
   of me.
This lesson I've learned from
   a lot of living:
The best about best isn't
   getting but giving.
        —Richard Armour.

Two-Way Truth
Eternal vigilance may be
the price of freedom but it's

also the mark of a nosy
neighbor.
        —Robert Fuoss.

Short Cut
Nowadays a lot of people
seem to learn the tricks of a
trade without learning the
trade.
        —H. E. Martz.

Headlines I Dream Of
"Postmaster-General
Announces Slash in Postage
Rates."
   "Doctors Claim Overweight
People Live Longer."
   "Pravda Accuses Viet Cong
of Atrocities."
   "National Budget Balanced;
Refund Due Taxpayers."
   "Designers See No Change
in Styles for Five Years."
        —Frank Rose.

Merely Asking
"We're here in this world to
   help others!"
I've heard this refrain o'er
   and o'er;
If it's true that we're here to
   help others—
Then what are the others
   here for?
        —F. G. Kernan.

Trick Record
"Honesty is the best policy"
To some has a hollow ring;

Truth: Hits, Misses and Errors

According to their ethics
It seems that the ploy's the
   thing!
          —G. O. Ludcke.

Ask Any Home Owner
Self-reliance is what we develop waiting for the service men to arrive.
          —Edward Stevenson.

Short Story
With shortages of this and
   that,
We'll soon be short of shorts.
One thing I'm out of,
There's no doubt of:
To wit, I'm out of sorts.
          —Richard Armour.

Generosity Gap
Probably the reason we admire the persons who think before they speak—they give us a chance to say something.
          —Maurice Seitter.

Biblical Boo-Boo
When Noah built the Ark
He knew of the flood in
   advance,
So why wasn't he also
   foresighted enough
To swat both flies when he
   had the chance?
          —R. M. Walsh.

Evulution
Scientists refer to the creation of Eve as splitting the Adam.
          —Frank Tyger.

What's Up?
Many a question is raised
And sometimes, just for the
   spite of it,
It's raised so high that the
   answer
Never quite gets to the height
   of it.
          —Richard Armour.

Foul Mot
"Brain-washing" it is called,
But that term I'm disputing.
For from the bilge they wash
   it with
It's more like brain-polluting.
          —A. S. Flaumenhaft.

Truth Capsules
Martyrs claim that sympathy is too good to waste on others.
          —Arnold Glasow.

Tolerance often gets the credit that belongs to apathy.

People who are always hitting the ceiling are apt to be full of hot air.
          —Franklin P. Jones.

Starting Point
Success comes from
   perseverance,
Dedication, hard work and
   pluck;
But having these
   characteristics
Is strictly a matter of luck.
          —Arnold J. Zarett.

Does Anybody Win?
Nowadays, when your ship finally comes in, chances are its cargo will get ripped off by waterfront racketeers.
          —Edward Stevenson.

The Bright Side
The nicest thing about an egotist is that he never goes around talking about other people.
          —Honey Greer.

Timely Note
Nothing makes you so aware of the passage of time as the class reunion. Unless, of course, it's being double-parked.
          —Franklin P. Jones.

Airborne Ambivalence
It's hard to understand the airlines. First they frisk you for weapons. Then they serve lunch and pass out steak knives.
          —Don Gastwirth.

Truth: Hits, Misses and Errors

Man of All Seesaws
It's so hard to make up my
mind,
Difficult to get it all together;
Since I'm plagued by
indecision,
I'm permanently under the
whether.
—Gail Cooke.

No Enigma
The book you can't tell
by its cover is likely to be
the one the kids have been
playing with.
—Franklin P. Jones.

The Tender Trap
A man can fool all
women some of the time,
and some women all the
time, but what bothers a man
most is why he can't fool the
same woman the same way
all of the time.
—P. J. Lark.

Sure Sign
You can also tell the
uncommitted. They don't have
bumper stickers and there's
no message on their t-shirts.
—Edward Stevenson.

Burning Question
When I want to look
Like the pensive type
I always light up
My crusty old pipe.

And then, deep in thought,
I reflectively sit—
Wondering why
My pipe won't stay lit.
—Arnold J. Zarett.

Script Problem
One of the things that
annoys us most about graffiti
is our inability to remember
whether it's spelled with two
f's or two t's.
—Edward Stevenson.

Unisex Unlimited
[*"Jack the Ripper was a
woman, a former top sleuth
at Scotland Yard believes . . ."*
—*WSJ news item*]
Jack the Ripper, of actions
shady,
Could have been, I believe, a
lady.
Now they'll convince men, if
they can,
That Lady Godiva was a
man.
—Ramona Demery.

Candid Comment
There's no rest for the
wary.
—Frank Tyger.

Long and Short of It
They say a person puts on a
long face
When he's sad. This seems to
me sappy—

Unless, of course, he also
puts on
A short face when he's
happy.
—Richard Armour.

Wrong Sequence
No wonder life
Leaves us baffled at best—
Always the lesson
Comes after the test!
—Thomas Usk.

IX AGING AND MATURITY

Tempus Fidgets

"Somehow I never thought of them as ever getting old."

Health Food Deduction

I've tried all the vitamins, the
   Bs, C and E;
Plus lecithin, bran, even kelp.
For like Ponce de Leon I
   find I must own
That a man of my age needs
   some help.
So what's the result of these
   tests
That I've run?
What is the unvarnished
   truth?
In a word, these elixirs, these
Magical fixers,
Are a poor substitution for
   youth.
          —Robert Fuoss.

Age Before Booty

One advantage of growing
   old,
Or so I've said, and so I've
   been told,
Is saying, "That was before
   your time"
Or, "You wouldn't know, so
   much younger than I'm."
Or even, and with a trace of
   scorn,
"You were only a child" or
   "You weren't yet born."
As generals, admirals pull
   their rank
I pull my age, and my years
   I thank.
I may be a little stiffer and
   wearier,
But just for the moment I
   feel superior.
          —Richard Armour.

Tempus Fidgets

I Can't Face It
Mirror, Mirror,
Have a heart
Spare me that early
Morning start!
      —Thomas Usk.

Steady Disposition
He claims that there is an
    advantage
To being just past his prime:
He has a more even
    temperament—
Now he's grouchy all of the
    time.
      —George O. Ludcke.

Transposition
The difference between
    "You're good-looking" and
(I know how weird this
    sounds!)
The phrase "You're looking
    good" is
Thirty years and 30 pounds.
      —R. M. Walsh.

Kid Stuff
Maybe one of the things that
    make
Human nature less than
    alluring
Is all of us who have learned
    the art
Of aging without maturing.
      —May Richstone.

Candid Comments
    Your've reached middle
age when kicking up your
heels no longer seems to get
you off the ground.
      —Franklin P. Jones.

    I'm at that age where I
have nothing to do with
natural foods. I need all the
preservatives I can get.
      —Bob Orben.

Out Of Joint
Middle-age is that touchy time
    of life
About which is made such a
    to-do,
When you paint the town
    (with only one coat)
And your back goes out
    more than you do.
      —George O. Ludcke.

Doubtful Progress
As a youth I was cocky and
    self-assured,
Rebellious, sassy and cuffable.
But the years have gone by
    and I have matured,
And now I'm simply
    insufferable.
      —William Lodge.

A Matter of Growth
At twenty I was wise and
    had
Messages I oft unfurled;
So sure was I that I could

Reconstruct the whole wide
    world.

At thirty I was cooling off,
    Indignantly sitting back,
Gradually suspecting that
There was some wisdom I
    might lack.

At forty I was laying down
The law just for myself;
My genius I had begun
To put upon the shelf.

Now at fifty I search in vain
For just one-word profound;
The only thing of which I'm
    sure
Is that the world is round.
      —Lea Zwettler.

Age Signal
    Somehow or other, as we
get older, work seems a lot
less fun and fun seems a lot
more work.

Love Everlasting
Will he be true when you are
    old,
No longer lovely to behold?
Of course, for what else can
    he do—
By then he'll be as old as
    you.
      —Suzanne Douglass.

Middle Age Syndrome
Now the children have
    departed,
Independent, fully grown,

Tempus Fidgets

And I can finally get started
On some projects of my own.

For twenty years I put aside
Things that, despite creative
    thirst,
I had not seriously tried
Because the home and kids
    came first.

Now emancipated, free,
I stand alone and insecure,
Unable for the life of me
To remember what the
    projects were!
                —Alison Wryley Birch.

Oldtimer's Lament
    By the time a man gets
smart enough to watch his
step, he's too old to go
anywhere.

New Identity
    Calling someone "a man
of parts" used to be a
compliment. Now, however, it
may only describe a fellow
who has false teeth and a
heart transplant.
                —Robert Fuoss.

Smoke Signal
Don't admit that you're
    becoming a part
Of the senior citizen sector
'Til the candles on your
    birthday cake
Set off the smoke detector.
                —George O. Ludcke.

Slow Emotion
I know I'm getting older
When I'm lying on the beach
and bikini-clad young misses
Are within my easy reach.

Yet I close my eyes and
    slumber,
Not because the flesh is
    weak,
But because, to state it truly,
I am really past the peek.
                —J. C. Soule.

Mid-Life Strife
    Middle-Age is when you
can't hum or sing any of the
ten best-selling records.
                —Philip Lazarus.

Change of Taste
I used to thrive on gory tales
Of murder, incest, plunder,
Of sad-faced maids entombed
    alive
And heroes torn asunder.

But lately Dumas, Kafka, Poe,
Et al can't fill this hollow.
McGinley, Wodehouse,
    Armour, Nash
Are easier to swallow.

Though Sturm and Drang
    and hapless love
Were fine when I was
    younger,
Of late the lighter forms of
    lit.
Appease this reader's hunger.
                —Edith Ogutsch.

Celebrity's Service
I hate to admit
That it fills me with glee
To see a movie star
Who's aging like me.
                —Lynn David Pleet.

Progress Report
I'm out of the woods at last,
    I say,
And at first it is quite a thrill
—
Till I notice that though I am
    out of the woods
I'm also over the hill.
                —Richard Armour.

Ex-Lothario's Lament
Farewell, romance!
I've aged. I'm in the forty-
    zone;
And think far less of
    courtesans
Than cortisone.
                —John Kine.

Permitted Prejury
    "What's your age?" the
magistrate asked the lady.
"Remember, you're under
oath."
    "Twenty-one and some
months," she answered.
    "How many months?"
    "One-hundred-and-fifty,"
she replied meekly.

Tempus Fidgets

Party Line
We know we're over the hill when baby-sitting with the grandchildren is the only invitation we get for New Year's Eve.
—George Bergman.

Retirement Note
The wife of a man who had recently retired was asked how her husband kept busy. "Oh, he putters around the yard and mutters around the house."
—Arnold Glasow.

Ring Out the Old
Retirement is nearing,
And I'm plotting what I'll do.
Florida appeals to me,
And Mexico does, too.
I'll gamble at Las Vegas
Or maybe O.T.B.,
Or else I'll take a freighter
    trip
To lands across the sea.
But most of all I'm planning
Two deeds of joy and charm:
I'll go to bed when I want to
And I won't set the alarm.
—Robert Gordon.

Reduce Speed
Middle age is the stage at
    which we engage
In jogging or pedaling a bike
To slow down the approach
of the sunset years—
At a pace faster than we'd
    like.
—George O. Ludcke.

No Daylight Saving
When I see the way time
    flies
My heart is filled with sorrow.
It seems only yesterday
That today was tomorrow.
—Maurice Seitter.

Proper Setting
For Chippendale, for pewter,
For Duncan Phyfe I hunger.
(When I'm surrounded by
    antiques
It makes me feel much
    younger.)
—Robert Gordon.

Town Crier
Admittedly, I am content
To have passed the Age of
    Consent.
And believe a long past
    season
Brought me to the Age of
    Reason.
But don't tell me a secret,
No intimate confession,
For I am not even close
To the Age of Discretion.
—Gail Cooke.

Early Likeness
If you'd like to know how
    someone looked
Twenty years ago, don't guess—
Just refer to the photo of
    him
That's used in the public
    press.
—George O. Ludcke.

Bleak Forecast
The middle years mark that quiet, peaceful, pleasant period between completing the children's college education and starting to help with the first grandchildren. The middle years usually last from three to five months.
—Honey Greer.

Moving Story
I'm proud that through the
    years
My weight has kept its
    ground;
Now all it has to do
Is stop shifting around.
—Mimi Kay.

Movie-going Senior Citizen
Card or no card, who cares
If my ripe old age is known!
But have the courtesy, please,
To insist that my card be
    shown.
—May Richstone.

Counterclockwise?
The best advice to a person
In whom fear of age is
    beginning to mount

201

Tempus Fidgets

Is don't count the years—
Instead, make them count!
　　　　—Ruth M. Walsh.

Truth Capsule
　　Nothing ages you faster
than trying to prove you're
still as young as ever.

How's That Again?
What's so bad about growing
　　old?
Well, among other
　　suggestions,
By the time one learns a few
　　answers,
He's forgotten half the
　　questions.
　　　　—George O. Ludcke.

Numbers Dodge
Whether it's number of
　　birthdays,
Or the miles per hour you
　　drive,
It's hard to find anyone
　　who'll admit
Exceeding fifty-five.

Standstill
Can we bridge the generation
　　gap?
The chances are but scant
While the younger doesn't
　　want to
And the older can't.
　　　　—A. S. Flaumenhaft.

Daffynition
　　Little old lady: mini-mum.
　　　　—Robert Fuoss.

Elder Statement
　　Bernard Baruch once said,
"To me, old age is always 15
years older than I am."

Lines for a Fortieth Birthday
Though others may rage
At the onset of Age,
I'm snobbishly cheering the
　　start of it—
In view of the way
Youth's acting today,
I don't care to be any part
　　of it.
　　　　—E. V. Girand.

Baldness

Falling Out
I brush my hair back.
I'm neat as a pin.
I wish, though, that I
Could brush it back
In.
　　　　—Richard Armour.

The Arrangement
A young man finds it quite
　　an art
To coax his hair into a part;
But art gives way to strategy
When man and hair part
　　company.
He combs each strand across
　　his pate,
Or forward, to conceal his
　　fate.
The trick, I guess, is how you
　　view it;
He feels secure. I see right
　　through it!
　　　　—Ellie Womack.

Fallout
Think of it this way
And it isn't so horrid:
You're not losing hair,
You're gaining some forehead.
　　　　—William T. Hogan.

Hair Today
The prow of his brow is
　　thinning out,
His hairline's beginning to slip;

Baldness

He used to be proud of his
   crew cut,
But the crew is deserting the
   ship.
                    —George O. Ludcke.

Skin Game
Never buy a cheap toupee,
No matter its style or design.
I did and now I'm losing hair
That isn't even mine!
                    —R. M. Walsh.

Home Grown
I know a man who's in the
   midst
Of having hair transplanted.
I'm fascinated, week by week;
Toward him my stare is
   slanted.

What once was scalp, devoid
   of hair,
Has all the hair it's needing.
I'm watching what I've never
   seen:
A hairline that's reseeding.
                    —Richard Armour.

"I have a lock of your hair that your mother
gave me, if you'd like it back."

Friendship

Truth Dodger
Acquaintances who aren't
    sincere
Have most transparent ways
Of saying what I like to hear
And coddling me with praise,
While true friends candidly
    reveal
Whenever I've annoyed them
Just exactly what they feel.
That's why I avoid them.
    —Sheldon White.

Breaking Even
    The wife of a bankrupt financier was confiding in a friend. "Since my husband lost his fortune, half his friends don't know him anymore."
    "Too bad," the crony chuckled. "But what about the other half?"
    "Oh, they don't know he's lost it yet!"
    —Grover Jones.

Loudspeaker
He's known for saying just
    what he thinks;
Inhibitions? he hasn't any.
He could be described as
    "outspoken"—
But you'd have to add, "not
    by many."
    —George O. Ludcke.

"Has it ever occurred to you, Leland, that
maybe you're too candid?"

Friendship

Do You Agree?
Agreeable people,
I've come to see,
Are people who always
Agree with me.
　　　　　—Richard Armour.

View Finder
Bad taste is easy to define;
It's that which disagrees with
　　mine.
　　　　　—Shirley Mitchell.

Point of View
He preens and says he's
　　found his niche,
A self-complacent statement
　　which
Implies he's sitting pretty; but
His friends insist he's in a
　　rut!
　　　　　—Harold Willard Gleason.

Here Today
Friendship, power, money,
　　love,
With their satisfying glow—
We must learn to take them
　　as they come,
And especially as they go!
　　　　　—Thomas Usk.

Silver Lining
　　When his son, a
promising young medical
student, dropped out of
college, the father's friends
were sympathetic.
　　"Save your sympathy for
someone who needs it," the
man said cheerfully. "A lot of
good can come out of an
unfortunate event. For
instance, this has cured the
boy's mother of bragging."
　　　　　—Duane Dewlap.

Feathered Friend?
　　"If you don't mind,
Peters," the eminent
ornithologist frostily told his
host at a cocktail party, "I'd
just as soon you didn't
introduce me to people as
the 'famous bird brain.'"
　　　　　—Edward Stevenson.

Mixed Meanings
　　High-handed: When a
friend thinks he knows what's
best for us.
　　Perceptive: When we
know what's best for him.
　　　　　—Guy Marvin.

Dangerous Intervention
To come between a man and
　　his wife
They say is a way of risking
　　life,
But what makes you even
　　less a winner:
Come between a dog and his
　　dinner.
　　　　　—Colleen Stanley Bare.

Friendship
　　When two hunters were
approached by the game
warden, one of them
promptly took off into the
woods. When the warden
finally caught him, the man
handed over his license.
　　"But if you had this why
did you run?" asked the
bewildered game warden.
　　"Because my friend didn't
have one."
　　　　　—Thomas Henry.

Film-flammed
We spent the summer here at
　　home,
While friends left on all sides.
We'll spend the winter, I'm
　　afraid,
In looking at their slides.
　　　　　—Dick Emmons.

Thank You Note
Friends giving me help with a
　　job
Say, "Don't mention it," that's
　　true;
But I often find later on
That when I don't, they do.
　　　　　—Edward F. Dempsey.

Patio Predicament
"Just passing by, we can't
　　stay long."
Leastwise, so he says.
But if it's true, how come he

Friendship

makes
A beeline for the chaise?
　　　—Rosemarie Williamson.

Barometer
Fair weather friends give you a feeling of security. As long as they're around you know that everthing is all right.
　　　—Maurice Seitter.

Reading Matters
So you can read me like a
　book?
You've told me that for ages.
Well, if you can I only hope
You'll kindly skip some pages.
　　　—Richard Armour.

A Wristed Judgment
He says he's glad to see me,
But it could be just a line—
If I judge by our handshake
The pressure is all mine.
　　　—Maurice Seitter.

Ego Eye
Please change the faults I see
　in you;
How deeply I deplore them!
My faults? But they're so
　small and few,
Why can't you just ignore
　them?
　　　—Elinor K. Rose.

Taxing Truth
In this mercenary and venal
　age
One fact is ineluctable:
It's a true friend that takes
　you out to lunch,
Even though you're non-
　deductible.
　　　—G. O. Ludcke.

Bear With Me
In our friendly relationship
Please don't call a halt
Just because I'm impossible—
It is my only fault!
　　　—Thomas Usk.

Creativity

Poetic Justice?
A sonic boom is loud and
　clear—
It penetrates the atmosphere.
Yet, poetry should claim its
　place
In inner, if not outer space;
Though fourteen lines may
　not say "vroom,"
Let's hear it for a "sonnet
　boom"!
　　　—Rosemarie Williamson.

Getting Your Wordsworth
I pity those who think poetry
Is never any fun;
To some, a rhyme is the
　name of the game;
Tennyson, anyone?

The Long Count
According to critics, the
　theme of my verse
Isn't always very inspired;
And, at the same time, its
　meter and rhyme
Also seem to leave a little
　something to be desired.
　　　—George O. Ludcke.

Poet's Problem
I can write of stars above
And of the comets bright,
But no matter how I try,
I can't get the meteorite.
　　　—Cobby Ellen Falkoff.

Creativity

Mental Derailment
Ideas can be so elusive
That often it will seem
That I've lost my train of
    thought
Before it can pick up steam.
            —Edward F. Dempsey.

Novel Notion
Writers who think they
have something to say often
turn out to have nothing
more than a compulsion to
say something.
            —Robert Fuoss.

Daffynitions
Writer's block: blankruptcy.
            —Walter Anthony.

Prophecy: insight job.
            —Len Elliott.

"Barton, do you have something you want to
share with the rest of us?"

Affairs of the Heart

"So... tell me about yourself. Do you like frogs?"

Shop Talk

An elderly lady went to the yarn shop of a large department store and asked the sales girl for instructions for making a dog's sweater.

"How large is the dog?" the girl asked. When the old lady's description turned out to be vague, the girl added, "Perhaps you ought to bring the dog in."

"Oh goodness, I couldn't do that! It's to be a surprise for him!"

—Anna Herbert.

Love Is Blind?

Don't underestimate love at
    first sight.
You'll be thankful after
    reflection.
After all, how many of us
Could pass a second
    inspection?

—Ruth M. Walsh.

Machine Mated

There's the couple who met through computer cards; it was love at first sort.

—Shelby Friedman.

Confessions of a Cynic

I've stopped looking for the
    perfect love;
My approach to the heart is
    pedantic.

Affairs of the Heart

Love, I find, is a compromise—
I know I'm curably romantic.
        —Herb Gochros.

Advice to the Lib-lorn
When a man proposes to
a girl he can no longer ask,
"Will you be mine?" Instead,
he will have to say something
like, "Let's be ours."
        —Maurice Seitter.

Fair Warning
Whisper sweet nothings in her
   ear,
Smile sweetly and recite
   them;
But, though she be your
   dearest dear,
Think twice before you write
   them.
        —Avery Giles.

Creative Thinkin'
As Edgar Guest has written,
Or would have, had he
   known:
It takes a heap o' lovin'
To make a spouse your own.

It also takes, when writin'
Such folksy lines as these,
A heap o' leavin' g's off
And usin' apostrophes.
        —Richard Armour.

Daffynitions
Cupid: patron of the
hearts.
        —Raymond J. Cvikota.

Lover's quarrel: When
romance is temporarily out of
ardor.
        —Dana Robbins..

February Special
I'm proffering my heart to
   you;
It's slightly beat, but it's still
   true.
Though many springs have
   sprung in it,
You'll find that I'm still young
   in it.
And though it's lacking
   warranties
On auricles and arteries,
I truly hope you won't
   decline
This all-time bargain,
   Valentine.
        —G. Sterling Leiby.

Lotion Emotion
My after-shaving lotion's fine,
With all that outdoor scent of
   pine.
If ads are right, I've bought
   quite cheaply
What makes attractive girls
   breathe deeply
And throw themselves, with
   all their charms,
Into my eager waiting arms.
But if they close their eyes,
   all dreamy,
And for a moment do not
   see me,

Perhaps they're thinking not
   of me
But of a tall, pine-scented
   tree.
        —Richard Armour.

I Need You!
I need you to light the stars
And set the sun afire.
I need you to dark the night
And quench this wild desire.
I need you to hold my hand
Whenever I'm in doubt.
But right now, dear, I need
   you most
To take the garbage out.
        —Jeanette Mack.

Wisdom

"That's it, then. 'Never draw to an inside straight!'"

Chew on This
Those who have had the
    experience
Are the ones most likely to
    know:
A man begins cutting his
    wisdom teeth
The first time he has to eat
    crow.
                —George O. Ludcke.

The Bright Side
Mistakes aren't all bad.
They at least prove that you
were doing something.
                —Frank Tyger.

Mixed Meanings
Serenity: the ability to
take things in stride.
Unmotivated: the other
fellow's serenity.
                —Thomas Henry.

Sound Fact
Oh, there is something
    wondrous
About a noise that's
    thund'rous:
It's that a vacuum in a cloud,
Or in a man, is awfully loud!
                —Carl Thompson.

Carrier
A perfectionist is one who
takes great pains—and gives
them to others.
                —F. G. Kernan.

Wisdom

Digestion Note
Flattery, like some foods,
is filling as you lap it up. But
it doesn't stick with you!

Just the Type
How man hates admitting an
    error,
How he'd like to be perfect,
    seraphical.
Such errors as must be
    admitted
He'd like you to think
    typographical.
                    —Richard Armour.

Floggers of Speech
The strongest words are
often used in the weakest
arguments.
                    —H. E. Martz.

After Thoughts
I'm very good with a quip or
    a jibe.
I can hold my own in a
    diatribe.
I can banter words that will
    add a spark
And I've mastered the art of
    the barbed remark.
I can always win in a verbal
    fray—
But not at the time, of
    course; the next day!
                    —Jean Conder Soule.

No Protest
Philosophers, in their own
    shrewd way,

Point out that a nation's fall
Results, not as much from
    what evil men do,
As from good men, who do
    nothing at all.

Philosophy
It really is a mistake
To worry far ahead;
The truth is, one day at a
    time
Is quite enough to dread.
                    —May Richstone.

Dim View
Those who complain
With each day that passes
Must look at life
Through woes-colored glasses.
                    —Gail Cooke.

Confirming Data
Most men claim to seek the
    truth
And don't intend to deceive.
But what they really seek are
    facts to support
The things they already
    believe.
                    —George O. Ludcke.

Simple Solution
Consider the really amazing
    results
If children never became
    adults,
In fact if we stayed as we
    were at seven,
Wouldn't earth be a place a

little like heaven?
No graft, no corruption—how
    well we'd behave—
No wars, no muggings, no
    need to shave,
Too young for driving, no
    accidents,
No sin, only wide-eyed
    innocence,
No second childhood, the first
    would suffice. . . .
Scant chance for all this, but
    it would be nice.
                    —Richard Armour.

Character Analysis
If you want to really
know a man, study his
behavior with a child, a
woman, a flat tire, and when
the boss is away.
                    —Paul Harwitz.

Toy Box
The world is such a great big
    toy
It could be lots of fun
If directions were only
    included
On how to make it run.
                    —Ruth Boorstin.

Modest Oblige
Modesty is the art of
hiding your light under a
bushel without leaving people
completely in the dark.
                    —Franklin P. Jones.

Wisdom

The Quantum Leap
Take the Big Step when the
time is right:
If you miss it, take your
lumps;
Remember, you can't leap a
chasm
If you try it in two small
jumps.
—George O. Ludcke.

Two Sense More
Most folks have five senses.
That's par for the course.
The wise have two more:
Namely, common and horse.
—Ann Bys.

Instant Information
If there's anything better
than good advice, it's a good
scare.

Semantic Matter
Language is a wonderful
thing. It can be used to
express thoughts, to conceal
thoughts, but, more often, to
replace thinking.
—Kelly Fordyce.

Social Note
Charm stops working the
minute you're aware you
have it.
—Bill Copeland.

Adult Education
I'm learning, much to my
sorrow,
That nothing is quite as fast
As the speed with which
each tomorrow
Becomes a part of the past.
—Henry Barton.

Appraisal
Those who complain the
loudest about how the cookie
crumbles probably dropped it
in the first place.

Melancholy Truth
The best things in life are
free—but we're not always
interested in the best things.
—H. E. Martz.

Generosity
When you meet the man
without a smile, try giving
him one of yours.

Hunting party
The man who thinks
before he speaks isn't always
weighing his words.
Sometimes he's searching for
them.
—Maurice Seitter.

Lock Out?
Temptation usually comes
in through a door that has
been left open.
—Arnold Glasow.

A Good Point
We have heads for the
same purpose a pin has—to
keep us from going too far.
—H. E. Martz.

Muffled Tones
My still small voice of
conscience
Is really quite sad,
For it's down inside me
where
The acoustics are bad.
—Ramona Demery.

Fret Work
Worry is like a
rockingchair; it gives you
something to do—but it
doesn't get you anywhere.
—Lucille S. Harper.

Dear Featherless Biped
Man is a "political animal"
Per Aristotle's view.
A "Social animal" per
Seneca,
Who saw him as an animal,
too.

"A poor, bare, forked animal"
Was something that
Shakespeare wrote.
"Half dust, half deity"—
From Byron, a worthy quote.

"An intelligence in servitude
to
Its organs" was Huxley's
description.
"A god playing the fool"

Wisdom

Was Emerson's inscription.

But Mark Twain described
   him,
(And his words were the
   best),
"The only animal that blushes,
Or needs to," was his
   bequest.
             —R.M. Walsh.

Discodata
    The man who doesn't
know which way to turn is
probably learning the latest
dance.
             —Bert H. Kruse.

Truth Capsule
    We never get a second
chance to make a good first
impression.
             —Marie Post.

Confusion Capsule
    The trouble with not
knowing what you want is
that you don't know what
you've got when you get it.
             —Bill Copeland.

Gossip

"You drop a few literary anecdotes
about me, and I'll drop a few about you."

Gossip

All Ears
When someone says to me,
  "My dear,
There's something that you
  ought to hear!"
I lean in closer, knowing well
It's something that she
  shouldn't tell.
                    —Gail Cooke.

Candid Comment
  The difference between
news and gossip lies in
whether you raise your voice
or lower it.
                    —Franklin P. Jones.

  Don't burden your friends
with your troubles. Tell your
enemies. They will be
delighted.
                    —Lucille S. Harper.

Daffynitions
  Scandalmonger:
prattlesnake.
                    —Doris Dolphin.

  Gossip: Wither report.
          —Raymond J. Cvikota.

Grandma Bell
Wire-tapping scandals
Shock the nation,
By which they're labeled
An innovation.
But speaking of scandals,
Grandma did fine

With a plain old-fashioned
Party line.
    —Georgie Starbuck Galbraith.

Outgoing
Invasion of privacy
Worries many,
But it really doesn't
Bother me any.

You see, I like people,
Gossip and laughter.
Evasion of privacy
Is what I am after.
                    —Richard Armour.

Entrance Exam
When you enter the room
Does the conversation cease?
If it does the chances are
You're the conversation piece.
                    —Maurice Seitter.

All Told
Gossip is a dreadful curse,
A plague, a scourge, or even
  worse,
A sneaky, sordid nasty thing
And always oh so interesting.
                    —Donna Evleth.

Words of Mouth
A tongue is just a little thing
That weighs a tiny bit.
Then why do such a lot of
  folks
Have trouble holding it?
                    —Margaret Hillert.

Ink Stink
  Some people act like
blotters when it comes to
gossip—they soak it all in but
get it all backwards.
                    —Wilfred Beaver.

Fast Report
Good news travels fast
And gossip never did lag
When a rumor's new,
Someone can't wait to
Let the chat out of the bag.
                    —Gail Cooke.

Ear-full
  Gossips seem to live by
heard instinct.
                    —Raymond J. Cvikota.

Confidence Game
What you're called if you tell
  a secret
Depends on a small detail—
In high places it's "top level
  informant";
Down below, you're a
  tattletale.
                    —G. O. Ludcke.

"I understand you've written a book."

On Having Had Enough

"I'm sorry, operator, that you accidentally refunded my money. No, I'll not redeposit it, but if you'll leave your name and address, I'll mail it to you."

Don't Push

I quiver till I turn dark green
When someone says "See
   what I mean?"
And if he queries "Follow
   me?"
I look around for room to
   flee.
I suffer agony unplanned,
So please don't press me.
Understand?
          —Dow Richardson.

Contrary Wise

Here's to the irksome fellow
   who
Must always take an adverse
   view.
If I complain about the heat,
He moans of frostbite on his
   feet;
If I predict a lengthy drought,
He gets his boots and
   raincoat out,
No matter what my creed or
   tenet
He's automatically agin it;
Our views will never jibe, it's
   clear—
He's got a built-in disagreeer!
          —G. Sterling Leiby.

Fighting Words

I'd like to see him bite the
   dust
Who has an ever-ready
   "thrust."

No major problems will be
   solved

On Having Had Enough

By him who vaunts he is
  "involved."

When I hear wide-eyed men
  aver
That they're "committed," I
  wish they were.

I'll start a stamp-and-yell event
Next time someone spouts
  "relevant."

By me there'll be no quick
  adoption
Of anything described as
  "option."

And certainly I will not adopt
An "option's" half-pint brother
  "opt"!
      —A.S. Flaumenhaft.

Vocabuleery
I'm not in the group
That says "one fell swoop,"
You don't hear me baying
"It goes without saying."
And I'm not one who sings
"It was one of those things."
Then a guy I stay aloof of
Speaks of the "warp and
  woof of."
But my special candidate
For crucifixion
Says something "without fear
Of contradiction."
      —Dow Richardson.

Rear View
Blessed are they who have
  no opinion.
They don't have to argue
  and dicker.

But most of all, they can go
  through life
Without a bumper sticker!
      —Ruth M. Walsh.

The Last Word
Put "the bottom line"
At the top of the list
Of the overworked phrases
That wouldn't be missed.
      —A.S. Flaumenhaft.

Bottom's Up
Among over-worked
  expressions
(Of which there's quite a
  crop)
Currently, "the bottom line"
Is really at the top.
      —Phil Stewart.

Daffynitions
  Bores: The criminally inane.
      —Ralph Noel.

  Gripe: Moanologue.
      —Frank Tyger.

  Apathy: vigor mortis

  A fanatic: a bore with
enthusiasm.
      —Frank Tyger.

Matter of Opinion
People who ask my opinion
On local and worldwide
  affairs

Would please me far more if
  they didn't
Insist, then, on giving me
  theirs.
      —Richard Armour.

Flower Glower
  If you want to find out
what hate is, just try criticizing
the "love generation."
      —H. E. Martz.

No Golden Age
Could he return here,
  Socrates,
Viewing today's mediocrities,
Might ring for room service,
  aghast,
And order, "A double
  hemlock, fast!"
      —Ethel Jacobson.

Music to Be Mugged By
Though music may soothe
The savage breast
And cool an attacker's
Felonious zest—
A soupcon of Schubert,
A snatch of Scarlatti—
I'd rather rely
On a spot of Karate.
(In fact, my first lesson's
Tonight at eight,
If I don't get jumped
Between Walnut and State.)
      —Ethel Jacobson.

On Having Had Enough

Cold Shoulder
I stand by the side of the
    road, weary,
Watching cars hiss past, fly
    by, each leery
Of stopping to help me in
    my plight.
As day dwindles to dusk,
    approaching night,
I wait, wonder, sigh, feeling
    ill-fated.
Both my tire and I are
    deflated.
            —Colleen Stanley Bare.

To an Ex-Smoker
You've sworn off smoking,
    you aver,
No cigaret droops from your
    mug.
Your self-control is laudable—
But need you be so doggone
    smug?
            —Paul Tulien.

Unfinished Business
Things I begin never seem to
    get done,
Quickly a bore though they
    start out as fun.
Projects I plan, hot on the
    griddle,
Never go much beyond the
    middle.
Walls stay half-papered, books
    partly read,
As I semi-attack other things
    instead.

Even in writing, as hard as I
    try,
I get to a point where
    suddenly
    I—
            —Arnold J. Zarett.

Predictable
I may have a stubborn
Streak, to my sorrow,
But at least I know what
I'll be thinking tomorrow.
            —Thomas Usk.

Health Bulletin
    It's true that some people
don't get ulcers. But that
doesn't mean they aren't
carriers!
            —Arnold Glasow.

Self-Destructing
    A bore is someone you
like a lot when you first meet
him—until he talks you out
of it.
            —Daisy Brown.

Timid Query
    Why is it that bravery is
seldom rewarded, while
cowards seem to get all the
cringe benefits?
            —Paul McCall.

People's Preference
    ["Survey indicates public
wants more reporting of
positive happenings in the
news."—News note.]
The negative tone of
    headlines today
Has created an unpleasant
    tedium;
When people are quizzed on
    what they'd prefer,
Their response is "A happier
    medium."
            —George O. Ludcke.

Poetic License
I detest that breed of men
    who think
That poetic purity
Must be buried in
Incomprehensible obscurity.
            —Arthur Magill.

Could Be Worse
Being a has-been isn't so bad,
And I make this statement
    because
Being a has-been at least is
    better
Than being a never-was.
            —Richard Armour.

Ltd.
Some feel great esteem,
Others great respect.
Some heap lavish praise,
Others genuflect.
At times my own regard
Rests on weaker grounds—
My admiration now and then
Knows bounds.
            —Dow Richardson.

On Having Had Enough

A Matter of Record
I'll be pleased with my life
When Fate writes "finis"
If my name does not
Appear in Guinness.
—Merri Beth Soames.

Long Count
I sit back in resignation
And wait for them to begin it
When anyone starts their
    pitch with,
"Have you got just a
    minute?"
—George O. Ludcke.

Stop Right There!
When a letter starts:
"It may interest you to know,"
That's as far as I go.
And just let one begin:
"You've been recommended
    for—",
I read no more.
While if it opens with:
"Under separate cover—",
I don't hover.
—Dow Richardson.

Passing the Buck
There are people who tend
To make a suggestion
By always putting it
In the form of a question.
"Shouldn't you send—?", they
    ask;
Or: "Isn't it best to sort—?"
And suddenly you find
The ball is in your court.

Butt I have never liked
To be pushed to the brink,
So I always come back with:
"Well, what do you think?"
—Arnold J. Zarett.

Sign Language
    Posted in the window of a
restaurant that had been
criticized for its poor food
and service: "Please Enter
Before Knocking."
—Thomas Henry.

Flat Statement
Annoying it is how people
    revel
In using the much abused
    word "level";
At the college level his
    teaching's done,
While her level is the primary
    one;
At the trainee level many
    begin,
At executive level they're
    really in;
The income level goes up or
    down,
As does crime level in every
    town;
There's the level of sickness
    and of health,
The level of poverty and of
    wealth;
There's the level of water and
    air pollution,
The level of theft and of
    restitution;

There's the level of on-and-off
    stage nudity,
The level of culture and of
    crudity.
When I hear that word, I feel
    like the devil
And I act like one—and
    that's on the level!
—A. S. Flaumenhaft.

Mental Health Item
    Happiness is not having to
hear what happiness is.
—Robert Fitch.

Laugh Track

"MacDonald's Farm ee-eye-ee-eye-oh!"

Mixed Emotions
"Where's your sense of
  humor?" They ask
When a problem results in a
  frown;
But if you play it light when
  things don't go right,
It's, "What are you, some sort
  of clown?"
— George O. Ludcke.

Smile Check
The ultimate test of
whether you possess a sense
of humor is your reaction
when someone says to you
that you don't.
— Frank Tyger.

Prescription
The first essential of a
happy life is the willingness to
be amused.
— Bill Copeland.

Down With Clowns
["—People don't want to
laugh as much as they used
to. 'Being funny seems to be
out of style'."—WSJ news
item]
Do not chuckle, laugh or
  grin;
Being funny isn't in.
Flash that grimace, hold that
  frown;
Keep your risibilities down!
Try to keep a smile from
  showing

Laugh Track

At statements such as the
    foregoing—
To think that humor's bit the
    dust
Has me laughing fit to bust!
        —E. V. Girand.

Mixed Meanings

Pun: the lowest form of
wit.
    Clever word play: when we
think of one.
        —Frank Rose.

Hip Breed

Man is the only animal
that laughs. But then he's
also the only one who
understands what his fellow-
men are up to.
        —Franklin P. Jones.

Daffynitions

Joke files: Jest of drawers.
        —Frank Tyger.

Old jokes: Laughed overs.
        —Maurice Seitter.

Puns: cornography.
        —Raymond J. Cvikota.

Practical joker: one who
laughs all the way to the
prank.
        —Lola Schancer.

One for the Road

Humor can break the
    monotony
And also make time pass
    quicker,
For the driver on a long road
    trip
Who enjoys a bumper snicker.
        —George O. Ludcke.

Laughing Matter

He who laughs last is thought
    to have won,
As surely you've heard and
    well know,
But he who laughs last may
    laugh last because
At getting the point he is
    slow.
        —Richard Armour.

Pessimists vs. Optimists

Truth Capsule

Worry is the advance
interest you pay on troubles
that seldom come.
        —Lucille S. Harper.

Some men never hear
opportunity knock because
they're too busy knocking
opportunity.
        —Hal Chadwick.

Daffynition

Incurable optimist: hope
fiend.
        —Shelby Friedman.

Second Opinion

A lot of people never
know a good thing unless
another person sees it first.
        —Lane Olinghouse.

Daffynition

Pessimist: Man of the
glower.
        —Lane Olinghouse.

Stop, Look and Listen

Over-optimism, the cautious
    suggest,
Is something from which to
    refrain;
(The light at the end of the
    tunnel, they say,
Could be that of an
    oncoming train!)
        —George O. Ludcke.

Pessimists vs. Optimists

Instant Information

A pessimist is someone who goes to a Chinese restaurant and asks for misfortune cookies.

—Ola McCollum.

No Hero

I'd like to face danger
With a confident chuckle,
But whenever I swash,
I usually buckle.

—William T. Hogan.

Tinted

There is a Midwestern florist who advertises that he sees the world through glass-covered roses.

Day-by-Day

The passage of time has
    always been
A tyrant, and here's the tip-
    off:
Even the old desk calendar
Is really a daily rip-off.

—George O. Ludcke.

Verbal Play

"We've got a dummy corporation.
What we need is a smarty corporation."

Secret Weapon
To get a word in edgewise in some crowds, it's necessary to couch it in a pointed remark.
—Lane Olinghouse.

Bell Song
Show me a bird that follows other birds to Capistrano and I'll show you a bird under the influence of a few swallows!
—Shelby Friedman.

No Title
Since brevity's the soul of wit, I quit.
—Dick Emmons.

Night Howl
Show me someone who habitually oversleeps and I'll show you cause for alarm.
—Bert Murray.

Forced Landing
"Now what's wrong with you?" a man asked his disconsolate-looking friend. "Just a little while ago you were on Cloud Nine."
"I know," sighed the friend, "I got air sick."
—Edward Stevenson.

Verbal Play

Candid Comment
People are far from perfect
—but they often seem perfect
from far.
—Frank Tyger.

The Eyes Have It
Ben Franklin had an eye for
the ladies
And an eye for the common
man,
And the better to see
Them both may be
The reason bifocals began.
—Richard Armour.

Bolt of Truth
It's easy to figure why
lightning never strikes twice; it
doesn't have to.

Commercially Speaking
For a dermatologist, booty
is skin deep.
—Raymond J. Cvikota.

No Horsing Around
This I have known for a
long, long time
And at last I am going to
say:
When you get it straight from
the horse's mouth
The chances are good it is
neigh.
—Richard Armour.

Pronounced Success
Some, rhyming it with
European,
Pronounce it proudly
Caribbean,
While others, rhyming with
amphibian,
Are just as sure it's
Caribbean,
Each thinks the other is
illiterate.
Such things as this they grow
quite bitter at.

I, being often wrong—hence
wary—
Have checked it in a
dictionary
Which, hoping to avoid a
fight,
Decides it this way: Both are
right.
—Richard Armour.

Good for Nodding
The reason so many
people tense up at auctions
might be that the auctioneer
looks forbidding.
—Pru Pratt.

Temperature Reading
Anybody who's always
cooling his heels probably has
cold feet.
—Franklin P. Jones.

Me and Plato
"Meaningful Dialogue," I'm
here to say,
Is any discussion where I get
my way.
—Herbert Warfel.

Reverse
[*"Old principals never die,
they just lose their faculties,"*
—*"Pepper and Salt.*]
Old faculties never die,
They just lose their principals.
—W. Glenn Mayes.

Pilot's License
On church bulletin board:
"Going to heaven? Get your
flight instructions here."

Words to Slip By
When I consider any word
High on the lists of those
misspelled,
I realize I'm the bird
Who, by these words, has oft
been felled.

No, they don't bother me,
and so
In turn, I've not annoyed
them;
It's not that I'm so smart,
you know—
It's just that I avoid them.
—G. Sterling Leiby.

Verbal Play

Ta Ta Tut
"So long, Pharaoh,"
Said the great god Osiris.
"Be seeing you
In the funny papyrus."
—Warren Knox.

Damp Investment
Buying a yacht is one way
of casting your bread upon
the waters.
—Frank Rose.

Daffy Dialogue
Sighed the girl dervish to
the boy dervish: "We live in
two different whirls!"
—Shelby Friedman.

Daffynitions
Solitude: conversation
peace.

Will power: a stop in the
right direction.

Sarcasm: quip lash.

Conformity: doing it the
herd way.

Buried treasure: sleeping
booty.

Argument: The steam of
consciousness.

Tranquility: rant control.

Inhibition: Trait jacket.

Promptness: Wait Reducer.

Ogler: peeromaniac.

Obscene phone calls: hide-
and-speak.

Secret opium crop: hush
poppys.

Seance: trance action.

Verbal Play

Word Game
"Prestigious" I am quick to
     use,
"In depth" I say with ease,
I toss off "ecumenical"
As well as "expertise."

So let me join your little
     group.
How happy you will be
To hear me speak of
     "dialogue"
And "serendipity."

You'll find me really quite
     reliable.
I use "charisma," too, and
     "viable."
            —Richard Armour.

Gin and Geology
Those drinks we label "on
     the rocks,"
My Stone Age friend reports,
Received that tag away back
     when
Folks drank 'em by the
     quartz.
            —Ralph Noel.

Fish Story
Of herrings there is none
     that's hipper
That he who is his brother's
     kipper.
            —Pru Pratt.

Oriented Expressed
This is not 1972,
Say the Chinese, that's an
     illusion;
They claim it's 4669 (Year of
     the Rat),
But to me, that's very
     Confucian.
            —G. O. Ludcke.

Philosophical Note
   It's true that life expectancy
is increasing: We can expect
just about anything these
days!
            —Arnold Glasow.

Language Lesson
Proper English
Doesn't always make sense;
But imperfect pasts
Make futures tense.
            —Ruth M. Walsh.

Poetic License
In a Gaelic mood I'll limn a
     limerick,
And sometimes I'll work up a
     sonnet,
Or delve into double dactyl—
When I can concentrate on it.

From coining a couplet when
     in my cups,
I find that it's hard to refrain,
And instead of an ode, I'd
     rather explode
With a quaint Quixotic
     quatrain.

I've been known to dabble in
     doggerel
(That's four-footed meter—and
     terse)
When some tell me that
     rhyme is a vast waste of
     time,
I reply that it could be verse.
            —G.O. Ludcke.

Ghost Slip
   I had a joke about the
Bermuda Triangle—but it
disappeared.

Cooking Lesson
I must confess I don't know
     why
We speak of children as small
     fry.
Adults, however, I've known
     toasted
And then a few days later
     roasted.
Still others I have often
     viewed
Hard boiled, half baked, and
     even stewed.
            —Richard Armour.

Of All the Gauls!
Caesar's legions, so we're
     told,
Were famous for their
     marches,
Which may account for Rome
     today
Being full of fallen arches.
            —Rosemarie Williamson